First World War
and Army of Occupation
War Diary
France, Belgium and Germany

47 DIVISION
Headquarters, Branches and Services
General Staff
1 June 1915 - 16 May 1916

WO95/2697B

The Naval & Military Press Ltd
www.nmarchive.com
Published in association with The National Archives

Published by

The Naval & Military Press Ltd

Unit 10 Ridgewood Industrial Park,

Uckfield, East Sussex,

TN22 5QE England

Tel: +44 (0) 1825 749494

www.naval-military-press.com

www.nmarchive.com

This diary has been reprinted in facsimile from the original. Any imperfections are inevitably reproduced and the quality may fall short of modern type and cartographic standards.

© **Crown Copyright**
Images reproduced by permission of The National Archives, London, England, 2015.

Contents

Document type	Place/Title	Date From	Date To
Heading	G. S. 47th Division June 1915		
Miscellaneous	47th Division.		
Heading	WO95/Stray/DDD		
Miscellaneous	D.A.G. 3rd Echelon Base		
Miscellaneous	G.O.C. 47th Division.		
Miscellaneous	D.A.G. 3rd Echelon Base	01/07/1915	01/07/1915
Miscellaneous	G R 741 7/6		
Miscellaneous	47th (London) Division.	01/07/1915	01/07/1915
Miscellaneous	47th (London) Division Situation On 3rd June, 1915	03/06/1915	03/06/1915
Miscellaneous	Positions Etc Of 47th Division Artillery	03/06/1915	03/06/1915
Miscellaneous	47th (London) Division.	03/06/1915	03/06/1915
Miscellaneous	47th (London) Division.		
Miscellaneous	47th (London) Division.	09/06/1915	09/06/1915
Miscellaneous	47th (London) Division.	10/06/1915	10/06/1915
Miscellaneous	47th (London) Division.	01/07/1915	01/07/1915
Miscellaneous	Defence Scheme "W" And "X" Sections.		
Miscellaneous	47th Div.		
Miscellaneous	1st Army No. 238 (G).	11/06/1915	11/06/1915
Miscellaneous	1st Corps.	13/06/1915	13/06/1915
Miscellaneous	Appendix. Notes By 142nd Infantry Brigade.		
Operation(al) Order(s)	Operation Order No. 24 By Lieut. General Sir. H. S. Rawlinson, Bart., K. C. B. C. V. O., Commanding IVth Army Corps.	07/06/1915	07/06/1915
Miscellaneous	47th Div. Arty.		
Miscellaneous	HQ 47th Div.		
Miscellaneous	A Form. Messages And Signals.	09/06/1915	09/06/1915
Miscellaneous		09/06/1915	09/06/1915
Miscellaneous	A Form. Messages And Signals.		
Miscellaneous	A Form. Messages And Signals.	10/06/1915	10/06/1915
Miscellaneous	A Form. Messages And Signals.		
Miscellaneous	A Form. Messages And Signals.	10/06/1915	10/06/1915
Miscellaneous	Advanced 1st Army.	10/06/1915	10/06/1915
Miscellaneous	Senders No. G. R. 810		
Miscellaneous	A Form. Messages And Signals.	10/06/1915	10/06/1915
Miscellaneous	Operations, June 13th, Etc.	12/06/1915	12/06/1915
Miscellaneous	Suggested Programme.		
Miscellaneous	Programme 47th Division.	13/06/1915	13/06/1915
Miscellaneous	Record Of Conference	11/06/1915	11/06/1915
Miscellaneous	47th Div.		
Miscellaneous	A Form. Messages And Signals.		
Miscellaneous	47th Division.	11/06/1915	11/06/1915
Miscellaneous	7th Division.	11/06/1915	11/06/1915
Miscellaneous	47th Div. Arty.	12/06/1915	12/06/1915
Miscellaneous	A Form. Messages And Signals.	11/06/1915	11/06/1915
Miscellaneous	47th Div. Arty.		
Miscellaneous	A Form. Messages And Signals.		
Miscellaneous	A Form. Messages And Signals.	12/06/1915	12/06/1915
Miscellaneous	C Form (Duplicate) Messages And Signals.	12/06/1915	12/06/1915
Miscellaneous	A Form. Messages And Signals.	13/06/1915	13/06/1915
Miscellaneous	A Form. Messages And Signals.		

Miscellaneous	Report On T. M. Attack 15/6/15		
Miscellaneous	Report Of Trench Mortar Attack		
Miscellaneous	A Form. Messages And Signals.		
Miscellaneous	140th Inf. Bde.	15/06/1915	15/06/1915
Miscellaneous	A Form. Messages And Signals.	16/06/1915	16/06/1915
Miscellaneous	A Form. Messages And Signals.		
Miscellaneous	C Form (Duplicate) Messages And Signals.		
Miscellaneous	A Form. Messages And Signals.		
Miscellaneous	A Form. Messages And Signals.	01/06/1915	01/06/1915
Miscellaneous	C Form (Duplicate) Messages And Signals.	01/06/1915	01/06/1915
Miscellaneous	A Form. Messages And Signals.	01/06/1915	01/06/1915
Miscellaneous	A Form. Messages And Signals.		
Miscellaneous	C Form (Duplicate) Messages And Signals.		
Miscellaneous	C Form (Duplicate) Messages And Signals.	01/06/1915	01/06/1915
Miscellaneous	47th (London) Division.	01/06/1915	01/06/1915
Miscellaneous	C Form. (Duplicate) Messages And Signals.	02/06/1915	02/06/1915
Miscellaneous	A Form. Messages And Signals.	02/06/1915	02/06/1915
Miscellaneous	C Form (Duplicate) Messages And Signals.	02/06/1915	02/06/1915
Miscellaneous	A Form Messages And Signals.	02/06/1915	02/06/1915
Miscellaneous	C Form (Duplicate) Messages And Signals.	02/06/1915	02/06/1915
Miscellaneous	Divisional Mounted Troops	03/06/1915	03/06/1915
Miscellaneous	47th (London) Division.	03/06/1915	03/06/1915
Miscellaneous	47th (London) Division.	04/06/1915	04/06/1915
Miscellaneous		05/06/1915	05/06/1915
Miscellaneous	A Form. Messages And Signals.	05/06/1915	05/06/1915
Miscellaneous	C Form (Duplicate) Messages And Signals.	05/06/1915	05/06/1915
Miscellaneous	C Form (Duplicate) Messages And Signals.		
Miscellaneous	A Form. Messages And Signals.	05/06/1915	05/06/1915
Miscellaneous			
Miscellaneous	Senders No. G. R. 702	05/06/1915	05/06/1915
Miscellaneous	47th (London) Division.		
Miscellaneous	47th (London) Division	05/06/1915	05/06/1915
Miscellaneous	A Form. Messages And Signals.	05/06/1915	05/06/1915
Miscellaneous	A Form. Messages And Signals.	06/06/1915	06/06/1915
Miscellaneous	Senders No. G. W. 724	06/06/1915	06/06/1915
Miscellaneous	47th (London) Division.	06/06/1915	06/06/1915
Miscellaneous	A Form. Messages And Signals.		
Miscellaneous	A Form. Messages And Signals.	07/06/1915	07/06/1915
Miscellaneous	C Form (Duplicate) Messages And Signals.	07/06/1915	07/06/1915
Miscellaneous	A Form. Messages And Signals.	07/06/1915	07/06/1915
Miscellaneous	47th (London) Division.	07/06/1915	07/06/1915
Miscellaneous	A Form. Messages And Signals.	08/06/1915	08/06/1915
Miscellaneous	C Form (Duplicate) Messages And Signals.	08/06/1915	08/06/1915
Miscellaneous	A Form. Messages And Signals.	08/06/1915	08/06/1915
Miscellaneous	Senders No G. W. 771		
Miscellaneous	C Form (Duplicate) Messages And Signals.	08/06/1915	08/06/1915
Miscellaneous	47th (London) Division T. F.	08/06/1915	08/06/1915
Miscellaneous	47th (London) Division.	09/06/1915	09/06/1915
Miscellaneous	C Form (Duplicate) Messages And Signals.	09/06/1915	09/06/1915
Miscellaneous	A Form. Messages And Signals		
Miscellaneous	47th (London) Division.	10/06/1915	10/06/1915
Miscellaneous	A Form. Messages And Signals.	11/06/1915	11/06/1915
Miscellaneous	47th (London) Division.	11/06/1915	11/06/1915
Miscellaneous	C Form (Duplicate) Messages And Signals.	12/06/1915	12/06/1915
Miscellaneous	A Form. Messages And Signals.		
Miscellaneous			

Miscellaneous	47th (London) Division.	12/06/1915	12/06/1915
Miscellaneous	Messages And Signals.	12/06/1915	12/06/1915
Miscellaneous	C Form (Duplicate) Messages And Signals.		
Miscellaneous	C Form (Duplicate) Messages And Signals.	13/06/1915	13/06/1915
Miscellaneous	47th (London) Division.	13/06/1915	13/06/1915
Miscellaneous	47th (London) Division.		
Miscellaneous	A Form. Messages And Signals.	14/06/1915	14/06/1915
Miscellaneous	A Form. Messages And Signals.		
Miscellaneous	47th (London) Division.	14/06/1915	14/06/1915
Miscellaneous	C Form (Duplicate) Messages And Signals.	15/06/1915	15/06/1915
Miscellaneous	C Form (Duplicate) Messages And Signals.		
Miscellaneous	C Form (Duplicate) Messages And Signals.	15/06/1915	15/06/1915
Miscellaneous	C Form (Duplicate) Messages And Signals.		
Miscellaneous	A Form. Messages And Signals.	15/06/1915	15/06/1915
Miscellaneous	C Form (Duplicate) Messages And Signals.	15/06/1915	15/06/1915
Miscellaneous	C Form (Duplicate) Messages And Signals.		
Miscellaneous	C Form (Duplicate) Messages And Signals.	15/06/1915	15/06/1915
Miscellaneous	47th (London) Division.	15/06/1915	15/06/1915
Miscellaneous	C Form (Duplicate) Messages And Signals.	16/06/1915	16/06/1915
Miscellaneous	C Form (Duplicate) Messages And Signals.		
Miscellaneous	A Form Messages And Signals.	16/06/1915	16/06/1915
Miscellaneous	C Form (Duplicate) Messages And Signals.	16/06/1915	16/06/1915
Miscellaneous	C Form (Duplicate) Messages And Signals.		
Miscellaneous	A Form. Messages And Signals.	16/06/1915	16/06/1915
Miscellaneous	C Form (Duplicate) Messages And Signals.	16/06/1915	16/06/1915
Miscellaneous	C Form (Duplicate) Messages And Signals.		
Miscellaneous	A Form. Messages And Signals.	16/06/1915	16/06/1915
Miscellaneous	C Form (Duplicate) Messages And Signals.	16/06/1915	16/06/1915
Miscellaneous	47th (London) Division.	16/06/1915	16/06/1915
Miscellaneous	C Form (Duplicate) Messages And Signals.	17/06/1915	17/06/1915
Miscellaneous	A Form. Messages And Signals.	17/06/1915	17/06/1915
Miscellaneous	C Form (Duplicate) Messages And Signals.	17/06/1915	17/06/1915
Miscellaneous	A Form. Messages And Signals.	17/06/1915	17/06/1915
Miscellaneous	C Form (Duplicate) Messages And Signals.	17/06/1915	17/06/1915
Miscellaneous	47th (London) Division.	17/06/1915	17/06/1915
Miscellaneous	A Form. Messages And Signals.	18/06/1915	18/06/1915
Miscellaneous	C Form (Duplicate) Messages And Signals.	18/06/1915	18/06/1915
Miscellaneous	47th (London) Division.	18/06/1915	18/06/1915
Miscellaneous	C Form (Duplicate) Messages And Signals.	19/06/1915	19/06/1915
Miscellaneous	A Form. Messages And Signals.		
Miscellaneous	C Form (Duplicate) Messages And Signals.		
Miscellaneous	A Form. Messages And Signals.	19/06/1915	19/06/1915
Miscellaneous	47th (London) Division.	19/06/1915	19/06/1915
Miscellaneous	A Form. Messages And Signals.	20/06/1915	20/06/1915
Miscellaneous	47th (London) Division.	20/06/1915	20/06/1915
Miscellaneous	A Form. Messages And Signals.	20/06/1915	20/06/1915
Miscellaneous	C Form (Duplicate) Messages And Signals.	21/06/1915	21/06/1915
Miscellaneous	A Form. Messages And Signals.	21/06/1915	21/06/1915
Miscellaneous	C Form (Duplicate) Messages And Signals.	21/06/1915	21/06/1915
Miscellaneous	47th (London) Division.	21/06/1915	21/06/1915
Miscellaneous			
Miscellaneous	C Form (Duplicate) Messages And Signals.	22/06/1915	22/06/1915
Miscellaneous	47th (London) Division.	22/06/1915	22/06/1915
Miscellaneous	C Form (Duplicate) Messages And Signals.	23/06/1915	23/06/1915
Miscellaneous	47th (London) Division.	23/06/1915	23/06/1915
Miscellaneous	C Form (Duplicate) Messages And Signals.	24/06/1915	24/06/1915

Miscellaneous	47th (London) Division.	24/06/1915	24/06/1915
Miscellaneous	C Form (Duplicate) Messages And Signals.	25/06/1915	25/06/1915
Miscellaneous	47th (London) Division.	25/06/1915	25/06/1915
Operation(al) Order(s)	47th (London) Division Operation Order No. 10	26/06/1915	26/06/1915
Miscellaneous	C Form. (Duplicate) Messages And Signals.	26/06/1915	26/06/1915
Miscellaneous	47th (London) Division	26/06/1915	26/06/1915
Miscellaneous	C Form (Duplicate) Messages And Signals.	27/06/1915	27/06/1915
Miscellaneous	C Form (Duplicate) Messages And Signals.	28/06/1915	28/06/1915
Miscellaneous			
Miscellaneous	C Form (Duplicate) Messages And Signals.	28/06/1915	28/06/1915
Operation(al) Order(s)	47th (Lon) Division Operation Order No. 11	28/06/1915	28/06/1915
Miscellaneous	47th (London) Division.	28/06/1915	28/06/1915
Miscellaneous	A Form. Messages And Signals.	29/06/1915	29/06/1915
Miscellaneous	C Form (Duplicate) Messages And Signals.	29/06/1915	29/06/1915
Miscellaneous	47th (London) Division	29/06/1915	29/06/1915
Miscellaneous	A Form. Messages And Signals.	30/06/1915	30/06/1915
Miscellaneous	47th (London) Division	30/06/1915	30/06/1915
Operation(al) Order(s)	Operation Order No. 29 By Lieut-General Sir H. S. Rawlinson Bt. K.C.B. C.V.O. Commanding IVth Army Corps	26/06/1915	26/06/1915
Miscellaneous	March Table		
Operation(al) Order(s)	1st Corps Operation Order No. 90	26/06/1915	26/06/1915
Miscellaneous	March Table For Movements 27th And 29th June 1915		
Miscellaneous	1st Div		
Miscellaneous	A Form. Messages And Signals.	27/06/1915	27/06/1915
Operation(al) Order(s)	1st Corps Operation Order No. 91	27/06/1915	27/06/1915
Operation(al) Order(s)	Operation Order No 50 By Lieut. General Sir H.S. Rawlinson Bt., K.C.B. C.V.O. Commanding 4th Army Corps.	27/06/1915	27/06/1915
Operation(al) Order(s)	1st Corps Operation Order No. 92	29/06/1915	29/06/1915
Miscellaneous	47th Division		

G. S. 47th DIVISION

JUNE

1 9 1 5

Situation Reports.

Tactical Progress Reports.

Orders & Instructions for
    Operations of 15th.

Defence Scheme.

SECRET.   47th Divn. G/111/2.
                                         Copy No.

47th DIVISION.

Principles for Defence of FESTUBERT ("C" Section).

General principles.
1. (a). The front line of trenches or breastworks to be held at all costs.

(b). Should any portion of the front line be broken, the remainder of the line will hold on.

(c). Local counter attack will be delivered at once to regain any of the line temporarily lost. Should this prove insufficient it will hold on to whatever line it makes good until counter attack by Brigade or, if necessary, Divisional Reserve can be delivered.

The infantry are therefore disposed in two main divisions :-

(i). For defensive action :-

   (a). Troops in front line trenches or breastworks, including those in their immediate support.

   (b). Garrisons of Supporting Points.

(ii). For offensive action :-

   Local battalion reserves.
   Brigade reserves.
   Divisional reserves.

Front line.
2. The front line must be capable of being fully manned without any delay, and cover must be provided for as many of the garrison as possible during a bombardment.

Supporting Points.
3. Supporting Points, constructed for all round defence, close in rear of the front line are to be permanently garrisoned. Their action, should the front line be broken, is to hold out to the last man in order to delay the further advance of the enemy, to fire on his attempts to establish himself on the ground he has gained, to break up his attack if he attempts to penetrate between the Supporting Points, and to assist the counter attack.
Garrisons of Supporting Points will NOT counter attack.

Counter attacks.
4. All officers will base their action on the established fact that the most effective counterstroke is that made by companies, always held in readiness to support the front line immediately the front line is broken.

Positions of reserves.
5. (i). Local reserves must be so placed that their offensive action can be set in motion without any delay. Rehearsals by day and night must therefore be held and the part which each is to play must be known to all ranks.

Cover

Cover from fire under which these reserves can be deployed must be so constructed as not to impede rapid offensive action across the open.

Communication trenches must also be provided up which they can be moved with the utmost rapidity, under cover, if time permits.

To assist their offensive, the ground in rear of the first line must be under the fire of Supporting Points in which <u>machine guns</u> are placed for the purpose, whenever available.

To add to the effectiveness of this supporting fire, entanglements should be prepared in rear of front line so as to break up the enemy's attack, if the hostile troops have been successful in crossing the front line, and to cause them to advance in directions which bring them under the fire of the Supporting Points.

(ii). Brigade Reserves are necessarily placed in accordance with accommodation available. They should be capable of turning out at short notice and will move to their place of deployment without further orders. It is therefore essential that the routes to be followed to the position of deployment are known and also well marked. These should be screened from view.

These reserves will be assembled in close proximity to the supporting line, viz - LE PLANTIN - FESTUBERT. From these positions, the exact site of which will be selected by the Section Commander, the Brigade Reserves are available to complete the action of local counterstrokes or, in case of extreme necessity should the enemy break through the line in strength, to occupy this supporting line which they would hold at all costs.

(iii). Divisional Reserves are maintained under the orders of the Divisional Commander for the purpose of a general counter attack in force in whichever section he may select. They are billeted some way back in order to ensure complete rest, but have rendezvous appointed to which they would move on receipt of orders. These rendezvous are known to Infantry Brigade Commanders.

Communications. 6. The essential factor for the maintenance of the front line is good communication, to ensure timely notice to the supports and reserves, to superior authority and to the supporting artillery, of any attack. It is the duty, therefore, of commanders to establish alternative methods of communication, and of all ranks to protect wires from damage. All officers must be made acquainted with the systems and, where necessary, telephone lines are to be <u>buried under the supervision of the signal service.</u>

Execution of works and R.E. 7. Every endeavour must be made to relieve the Royal Engineers of all work that can be done by infantry working parties.

All wiring, trench and breastwork can perfectly well be carried out by infantry, and it should be a point of honour with all ranks that they are independent of outside assistance for the execution of these works to which they are trained.

Brigade

Brigade workshops should be formed under the direction of the R.E. for the preparation of trench stores, including periscopes, masks, etc.

The Royal Engineers should only be called in for special tasks requiring technical knowledge or very rapid execution, and infantry brigade commanders, in consultation with the C.R.E., will see that the work required is explained at once, so as to allow of the preparation of the necessary materials without delay.

Royal Artillery. 8. Close co-operation with the infantry, the support of whom is their primary function, is essential for all battery officers. Their observing stations should be made known to relieving infantry and their requirements for observation under varying circumstances should be explained. These requirements will be completed in co-operation with infantry commanders.

The C.R.A. is responsible for complete and accurate registration and that the necessary data is always instantly available for fire to be opened when support is called for. He is also responsible for giving additional artillery support to any threatened point should it be required, and for the necessary registration having been completed, and further for arranging mutual support with neighbouring divisions.

Offensive action. 9. It is to be remembered that the surest defence is to maintain a continuous superiority over the enemy and this is attained by better snipers, more active patrols, keener listening patrols, and by constant reconnaissance of his front line and of any movement in rear of it.

Firing line. 10. Although loopholes may be used for snipers and although head cover is necessary for machine guns and their detachments, in case of attack every man will fire over the parapet. For this purpose constant supervision over the firing platform is necessary so that repairs may be made at once, and that the maximum number of men may be accommodated in the firing line.

Every man should be familiar with the exact spot which he is to occupy at the parapet.

Schemes of defence. 11. Sub-section commanders will study their areas and frame plans for action from the point of view of :-

(a). Any portion of their line being broken.

(b). The neighbouring sub-section being broken.

Their plans will show :-

(i). Normal distribution of the infantry.

(ii). Action by the infantry in case of attack.

(iii). Communication trenches or additional works or wiring required.

(iv). Rapid communications with brigade headquarters, neighbouring sub-sections, and supporting batteries.

(v)

(v). **Action by machine guns, including the preparation of alternative positions for them.**

(vi). Supply and storage of hand grenades, S.A.A., Supplies, and water. Care is to be taken that the stock of water should be constantly "turned over".

These plans will be co-ordinated by the section commander who will consult with the officers commanding the supporting artillery. Works to be carried out should be put in hand at once.

Similarly, the section commander will prepare plans, including proposed new works, and submit them to Divisional Headquarters, including in them the details of artillery support.

It is essential that all officers be intimately acquainted with the plans of the area in which they operate, and that all ranks should know beforehand what they are to do when they first take up their duties, whether as trench or supporting point garrison, or as part of the mobile supports, or reserves.

Great attention is to be paid to the proper maintenance and care of masks and of the solution of bi-carbonate of potash intended to neutralize the effect of poisonous gases.

No. G/111/2.

13th May, 1915.

Lt.Colonel,
General Staff,
47th Division.

Distribution :-
Copy No. 1. General Staff.
,, 2. ,,
,, 3. ,,
,, 4. ,,
,, 5. A.A.& Q.M.G.
,, 6. 47th Divl.Mtd.Troops.
,, 7. 47th Divl.Arty.
,, 8. 47th Divl.Engrs.
,, 9. 47th Divl.Sigs.
,, 10. 140th Inf.Bde.
,, 11. 141st Inf.Bde.
,, 12. 142nd Inf.Bde.
,, 13. 47th Divl.Med.

woas/strayl DDD

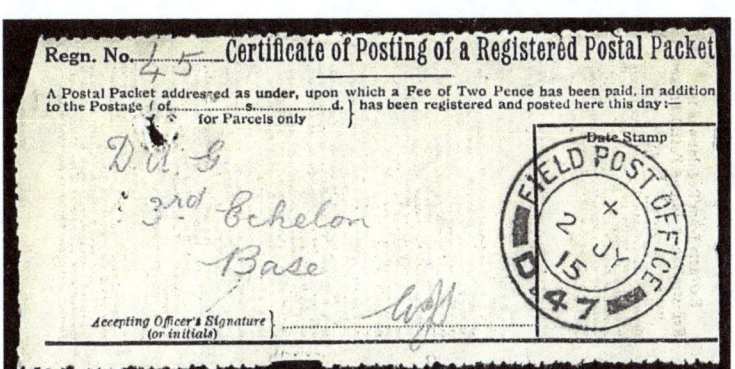

G.O.C. 47th Division

War Diary April 1915 Margin - forwarded under your memo G/51/3 of the 1.7.15 have been received.

The Documents referred to in the

[signature]
Captain,
D. A. A. G.
for D. A. G., 3rd Echelon.

A.G.'s OFFICE AT THE BASE
CENTRAL REGISTRY Base,
15 JUL 1915
C. R. No. 1440

G/81/3

D.A.G.
    3rd Echelon,
        BASE.
========================

    Herewith General Staff War Diary with Appendices, of the 47th (London) Division, for the period 1st to 30th June 1915, both dates inclusive.

    Kindly acknowledge receipt.

47th Div.G/81/3.   Major General,
1st July 1915.   Commanding 47th (Lon) Division.

6/6 3/6
5/6 2/6 4/6

7/6
GR 741
Pos u zutung
83¢ 11/6

Missing from affinities
Could not find them

47th (LONDON) DIVISION.

WAR DIARY - GENERAL STAFF

JUNE, 1915.

BETHUNE.   **1st June 1915.**

          Fine night.   Fine morning.

Time	Entry	Ref.
1-55 a.m.	6th London Battalion reported relieved by 20th Brigade. 15th Lon.Battn. relieved by Grenadier Guards.	
	140th Inf.Bde. H.Q. open at 8 Boulevarde Frederick De Georges, BETHUNE.	B.M.36. B.M.37.
7-30 a.m.	2nd Canadian Brigade will begin to relieve right Brigade of 47th (London) Division at 4-40 p.m. today.	G/655/Can.Div.
10-30 a.m.	1st Corps Hd.Qrs. closes at CHOCQUES at 3 p.m. today and opens at Chateau, LA BUISSIERE (J.4.c.8.2.) at same hour.	G/623/1st C.
	140th Inf.Bde. Sig. Sec. to relieve 1st Guards Bde. Sig. Sec. as soon as possible. G.O.C. 1st Guards Bde. to remain in his present H.Q. in command of sub-section until relieved by 141st Inf.Bde. Whole section under command of G.O.C. 1st Div. till 6 p.m. 2nd June. 1st Gds.Bde. can call on 140th Inf.Bde. if necessary.	G.H.613.
11-50 a.m.	Lt.Col. W. Thwaites, R.A. to command 141st Inf.Bde.	
	Lt.Col. The Hon. W.P. Hore-Ruthven, C.M.G., D.S.O., to be G.S.O. 1st Grade, 47th Division.	A.Q.596.
2-55 p.m.	47th Division to take over command of "Y" and "Z" Sections from 6 p.m. 2nd June.	
3-30 p.m.	140th Inf.Bde. to take over whole of Section "Y" from 6 p.m. this evening. This will include Y.3 and Y.4 now held by 2 battalions of 1st Division.	G/190/1st Div.
3-50 p.m.	Situation of Artillery Headquarters and units.	B.M/83.
4-20 p.m.	Headquarters 141st Inf.Bde. open at 8 Boulevarde Frederick De Georges, BETHUNE, at 7-30 p.m. tonight.	B.M.510.
9-0 p.m.	Adv. 2nd Div. Hd.Qrs. open at Chateau MAZINGARBE at 9 a.m. 2nd June. 2nd Div.Hd. Qrs. remain at Chateau LEZ CHARMEUX.	G/893/2nd Div.
	140th Inf.Bde. Hd.Qrs. opened at NOYELLES LEZ VERMELLES at 7 p.m. today.	B.M.47.

2nd June 1915.

BETHUNE.

Fine night – Fine morning.

1-20 a.m.	Reliefs in Y.1 and Y.2 completed.	B.M/120/140th B.
3-14 p.m.	141st Inf.Bde.H.Q. moves from BETHUNE and will open at CAMBRIN at 5-30 p.m.	B.M.529.
3-40 p.m.	142nd Inf.Bde. report situation of units.	B.M.703.
4-0 p.m.	47th Div.Hd.Qrs. closes at Level Crossing (E.4.a.7.5.) at 4 p.m. and re-opens at same hour at VERQUIN (E.29.b.2.6.).	G.H.626.
6-15 p.m.	G.O.C. 1st Division hands over command of "Y" and "Z" Sections to G.O.C. 47th Division.	G/208/1st Div.

3rd June 1915.

VERQUIN.   Nothing happened. Z.1.Section renumbered Y.4.

Situation of units.   .   .   Attached.

4th June 1915.

VERQUIN.

Fine night – dull misty morning.

5-30 a.m.	Quiet night reported.	
9-35 a.m.	7th Divn. captured I.2 and I.4 last night but were bombed out this morning.	(Telephone).
7-50 p.m.	Preliminary order for relief of 2nd Divn. issued to formations of 47th Div. (Secret).	
8-45 p.m.	2nd Divn. to take over 47th Div. line. Detailed orders later.	

5th June 1915.

VERQUIN.

Fine night. Fine hot morning.

5-30 a.m.	Quiet night reported.	
12-35 p.m.	1st Corps call for programme of reliefs according to 1st Corps Operation Order 88. Sent 2-12 p.m. . . .	G.R.698. G.676/1st C.
2-45 p.m.	Received Time Table for movements of 2nd Div.Troops through NOEUX LES MINES. .	G.943/2nd Div.
6-0 p.m.	140th Inf.Bde.ordered, on relief by 6th Bde., to send one battalion to LES BREBIS to come under orders of 142nd Inf.Bde.	G.W.700.
9-25 p.m.	One battn. 141st Inf.Bde. to move into LES BREBIS night 6th/7th to be at disposal of 142nd Inf.Bde. till night 7th/8th. . .	G.W.706.

3.

VERQUIN.   6th June 1915.

Fine night. Fine morning.

Quiet night reported.

7-55 a.m.   142nd Inf.Bde. informed that road through
NOEUX LES MINES available between 9-30 and 10-30
p.m. and not as stated in G.R. 703.   G.W.715.

10-0 a.m.   Command of sub-sections to pass to G.O.C's
relieving Bde. as soon as reliefs are completed.   G.H.716.

11-5 a.m.   200 spades and 150 picks to be kept in "W"
and "X" Sections.   G.H.719.

1-0 p.m.   2nd Div. propose that their C.R.A. should
take over Y.1 - Y.4 from 6 p.m. June 7th.
C.R.A. 47th Div. proposed to take over 2nd Div.
Section Artillery same date.   B.M.241.

5-0 p.m.   Alteration in Operation Orders G.R.702   G.W.724.

VERQUIN.   7th June 1915.

Fine night. Fine morning - very hot.

1-25 a.m.   Relief of 141st Bde. in Y.3 and Y.4 completed.   G.W.732.

2-0 a.m.   Reliefs in Section "W" reported complete. G.W.733.

5-30 a.m.   Quiet night, except for intermittent M.G.Fire.

11-35 a.m.   All Inf.Bdes. told they can draw S.A.A. from
any of the F.A.Bdes.Ammn.Cols.at DROUVIN WOOD.   G.R.741.

6-0 p.m.   Adv.2nd Div. closed at MAZINGARBE and
reopened at Chateau DES PRES at 6 p.m.   G.987/2nd Div.

6-45 p.m.   All ranks forbidden to approach batteries
in action. No officers to enter artillery
Observation Posts without permits from G.S.   G.H.754.

7-45 p.m.   Both batteries of Howitzers can be withdrawn
to reserve.   G.R.755.

8-0 p.m.   1st Corps ask that any heavy artillery
bombardment should be reported.   G.H.757.

8-35 p.m.   141st Inf.Bde.H.Q. moving to LE SAULCHY FM
(L.17.d)   Established at 10 p.m.   B.M.655.

10-30 p.m.   Germans seen near A.2, apparently experi-
menting with poisonous gases.   G.H.760.

VERQUIN.   8th June 1915.

Fine night. Fine morning.

1-30 a.m.   Reliefs complete in Section X and command
of section taken over by 141st Inf.Bde.   G.H.763.

                Much wheeled traffic heard moving South
from opposite L.8.   G.H.764.

8th June (contd).

1-45 a.m.	140th Inf.Bde.H.Q. opens at MAZINGARBE. Reliefs complete.	B.M.78.
8-0 a.m.	1st Corps orders arrangements to be made for co-operation of two 4.7 batteries with French XXI Corps on right. Wireless being placed at our disposal for this purpose.	G.713/1st C.
10-0 a.m.	1st Corps report that asphyxiating gas pressure pump has arrived at ILLIES. Sharp look-out to be kept.	G.714/1st C.
10-10 a.m.	1st Corps order gas proof M.G.Emplacement to be made early.	G.716/1st C.
12 noon to 12-30 p.m.	Enemy shelled North of Sub-Secn.X.2. Strong line of wire from M.11.a.19. to M.10.a.94. Enemy's line strongly wired from M.4.a.22 to G.34.c.78, especially near latter.	

VERQUIN.
9th June 1915.

Fine night. Fine morning. Thunder and rain during afternoon of 8th.

8-20 a.m.	140th Inf.Bde. report reserve M.G.Teams in all battalions.	M.G.92.

VERQUIN.
10th June 1915.

Fine night. Dull morning.

10-40 a.m.	Only traffic allowed on road running from Chateau MAZINGARBE to LE SAULCHOY FARM is that proceeding to Hd.Qrs.47th Div.Engrs., and French Arty.Comdrs.Hd.Qrs. No troops to drill in field S.E. of the road.	G.R.801.
11-55 a.m.	R.E. ordered to supply about 30 short scaling ladders for 142nd Inf.Bde.	G.R.803.

VERQUIN.
11th June 1915.

Rain during night. Dull morning.

6-45 a.m.	1st Corps call conference of G.O's.C. 1st, 2nd and 47th Divisions at VAUDRICOURT at 11 a.m. C.R.A's and G.S.O's to attend.	G.H.817.
	Enemy shelled sub-section X.1 during day.	

VERQUIN.
12th June 1915.

Fine night. Dull morning.

5-15 a.m.	Large german working party fired on opposite X.2., by 141st Inf.Bde.	B.M.758.
	Number of days in and out of trenches received from Inf.Bdes. List attached.	

12th June (contd).

	140th Inf.Bde. relieve 141st Inf.Bde. tonight, in Section "X".	G.H.851 of 11th.
	15th Lon.Battn. to remain with 142nd Inf. Bde. One battalion of 141st Inf.Bde. to be at disposal of 140th Bde. (battn.at PHILOSOPHE).	
3-5 p.m.	On relief tonight, 141st Inf.Bde. H.Q. will be at NOEUX LES MINES.	
	140th Inf.Bde.H.Q. remain at MAZINGARBE Chateau.	G.R.845.
10-10 p.m.	Battalions in Divisional Reserve to be ready to move at 2 hours notice.	G.R.859.
7-55 p.m.	German observation balloon up and able to see down street where reserve companies of X.1 and X.2 are billeted. It will be fired on tomorrow if within 10,000 yards.	B.M.783.
11-32 p.m.	Relief of 141st Inf.Bde. by 140th Inf.Bde. completed at 10-40 p.m.	S.G.339.

VERQUIN.   ### 13th June 1915.

Fine night.   Fine morning.

7-59 a.m.	Situation of units of 140th Inf.Bde.:- 6th Bn. X.1., 7th Bn. X.2., 8th Bn.PHILOSOPHE. 17th Bn(attached) - half PHILOSOPHE and half at MAZINGARBE.	B.M.127.
8-15 a.m.	Situation of units of 141st Inf.Bde. 19th and 20th Lon.Bns. at MAZINGARBE; 18th Bn. at NOEUX LES MINES. Bde.Hd.Qrs.- LE SAULCHOY FM.	B.M.791.
9-6 a.m.	142nd Inf.Bde. units disposed as follows :- 21st Bn. in W.1., 15th Bn. W.2., 23rd Bn. & 1 Coy.24th Bn. W.3., 22nd Bn. and remainder of 24th Bn. in Bde.Reserve at LES BREBIS.	B.M.760.
7-25 p.m.	141st Inf.Bde.H.Q. established at NOEUX LES MINES (K.18.b.4.3.).	B.M.801.
	During day enemy used trench mortars against W.1 and W.3.	
	Constant stream of traffic heard from 9-0 to 11-30 p.m. moving South from LOOS.	

VERQUIN.   ### 14th June 1915.

Fine night.   Fine day - cooler.

9-30 a.m.	When 15th Lon.Bn. is relieved from trenches on night 16th/17th, it will rejoin 140th Inf.Bde. and its place will be taken by a battn. of the 141st Inf.Bde.	G.R.867.
5-10 p.m.	Lieut.GAUTERON does not think Germans were mining or likely to mine under 142nd Inf.Bde.Area.	G.H.894.
8-45 p.m.	113th Batty.R.G.A. at disposal of 2nd Divn. not 47th Div.	'Phone.

14th June (contd).

11-50 p.m.   Bombing party of 15th Lon.Bn. attacked SNIPERS HOUSE. One German look-out man ran back. Germans manned their trenches. No casualties to our men.   ('phone).

VERQUIN.   ## 15th June, 1915.

Fine night. Fine morning - warmer.

10-0 a.m.   Bombing attack on German Sap opposite Sap 18. The attack started at 10-30 p.m. and had the effect of rousing the Germans who opened heavy rifle and shell fire and clearly had a large number of men in trenches. Sap destroyed in some places by enemy's shell fire. Sap obviously registered. No casualties.   B/645.

Report of Trench Mortar attack on Sap 12. Commenced at 10-30 p.m. Average of 9 rounds per Mortar fired in 15 minutes. Very little response except a little Machine Gun Fire. Sap apparently hit; also salient of German trench opposite left of battery.

12-40 p.m.   Certain amount of movement around LILLE, DON, etc. Probably reinforcements for NEUVE CHAPELLE Section. Unlikely to be more than one regiment.   G/793/1st C.

3-40 p.m.   142nd Inf.Bde. asked to consider and give an opinion on desirability of joining our line near Sap 18 with MAISON DES MITRAILLEURS, thus reducing length of line. Also asked for estimate of work required.   G.R/905.

5-37 p.m.   Scaling ladders and bayonets displayed in K.1. Enemy opened heavy shrapnel fire on K.1 and communication trenches. French Artillery replied effectively.   G.H/908.

6-0 p.m.   Message to Colonel Muller and French Artillery thanking them for work done in co-operation with 47th Division.   G.R/911.

8-10 p.m.   Observation Officer's report. Canadians have taken H.4,-H.15. 7th Div. captured first line and working up towards 2nd Line. 51st Division have reached N corner of RUE D'OUVERT and are bombing down it (not yet officially confirmed). Up till then no intense bombardment on our troops. 1st Corps attribute this to operations of 47th Division.   Confirmed 8-45 p.m.   G.H.912. G/797/1st C.

10-20 p.m.   140th Inf.Bde. report German scaling ladders distinctly seen opposite Sap 16. Great vigilance ordered.   S.C.518.

VERQUIN.   ## 16th June, 1915.

Fine night. Fine morning.

7-5 a.m.   Heavy bombing counter-attack compelled our troops to withdraw from positions gained last night North of Canal.   G/801/1st C.

16th June (contd).

9-35 a.m.	Detailed account of above from 1st Corps. 2nd Army report having penetrated German lines in several points from HOOGE CHATEAU - YPRES - ROULERS Ry.	G/802/1st C.
5-25 p.m.	1st Corps order that no reliefs are to take place tonight.	G.H./924.
6-25 p.m.	French reported to have captured front line of German trenches. French troops have reached ridge S.E. of SOUCHEZ.	G/808/1st C.
7-0 p.m.	4th Corps occupied L.10 and I.2 - I.4.	
7-20 p.m.	2nd Army report not much progress. German counter-attack failed.	G/413/1st C.
9-42 p.m.	141st Inf.Bde.H.Q. established at MAZINGARBE.	B.M.860.
10-40 p.m.	4th Corps have taken L.10 - L.8 - K.6 - J.10 and I.2 - I.4. Driven out of all except K.6 - J.10.	G/818/1st C.

VERQUIN.

17th June 1915.

Fine night. Fine day.

8-50 a.m.	6th Inf.Bde. no longer in Corps Reserve. 1st Guards Brigade remain in Corps Reserve.	G/823/1st C.
10-10 a.m.	Reliefs which were postponed last night may be carried out tonight.	G.H.937.
11-0 a.m.	141st Inf.Bde. will relieve 142nd Inf.Bde. in Section "W" on night 20th/21st June. 142nd Inf. Bde. will billet 2 battns at MAZINGARBE, remainder at NOEUX LES MINES.	G.H.938.
12-27 p.m.	Amendments to 142nd Bde.Operation Order No.22, received.	B.M.792
1-9 p.m.	141st Inf.Bde.H.Q. established at NOEUX LES MINES	B.M.868.
2-45 p.m.	Major Hermon, K.E.H., to take over charge of Divl.Bombing School, with effect from 18th June.	G.H.941.
3-9 p.m.	Battalions of 141st Inf.Bde. usually billeted at NOEUX LES MINES will remain for the present at MAZINGARBE. Working parties from brigades for tonight to be detailed as usual.	G.H.940.
6-40 p.m.	1½ in Trench Mortar Battery sent to 140th Inf. Bde. for "X" Section. 95 mm Trench Mortars now in "X" to be transferred to "W" Section.	G.H.946.
8-10 p.m.	1½ in T.M.Battery will reach 140th Bde. in morning instead of tonight as at first ordered.	G.H.948.
10-20 p.m.	Railway activity about LENS. All precautions to be taken against hostile attack.	G/851/1st C.

3.

VERQUIN.   18th June 1915.

            Fine night. Fine day.

8-59 a.m.   In event of hostile attack, working parties
                will not attempt to rejoin their own units during
                the attack unless they are working close to battn
                assembly place. They will attach themselves to
                the nearest unit.   . G.H.957.

5-55 p.m.   When reporting gun flashes at night, exact
                time should be stated.   .   . I.G/48/1st C.

VERQUIN.   19th June 1915.

            Fine night. Fine morning.

8-45 a.m.   1st Corps report unusual railway activity
                at LA BASSEE and DON about 4 - 5 a.m.   . G/849/1st C.

                                                                         G.R. 973
4-15 p.m.   Two 15 pr Batteries of 47th Div. will move
                into position night 20th/21st June and will be
                attached to 2nd Division.   .   . G/852/1st C.

9-0 p.m.   G.O.C. held conference of Brigadiers at   G.R. 980
                MAZINGARBE at 9 p.m.

10-15 p.m.   Relief of "W" Section arranged for night of
                20th/21st is postponed till night 21st/22nd.   . G.H.983.

                        20th June 1915.

            Fine night. Fine morning.

1-0 p.m.   G.O.C. orders conference of G.O.C., R.A.,
                C.R.E., and Inf.Brigadiers, at MAZINGARBE Chateau
                at 4 p.m. today.   .   . G.H.986.

6-0 p.m.   Relief of 142nd Inf.Bde. by 141st Inf.Bde.
                to be carried out tonight as originally ordered.   . G.W.991.

6-55 p.m.   Squadron K.E.H. to do 48 hours in trenches
                attached 141st Inf.Bde.   .   . H.H.992.

                        21st June 1915.

VERQUIN,   Fine night. Fine morning.

1-0 a.m.   Relief of "W" Section completed. Command of
                Section taken over by 141st Bde.   W.1 - 18th Bn.
                W.2 - 20th Bn., W.3 - 19th Bn. Bde.Res.- 17th Bn.
                Bde.H.Qrs. at K.18.c.3.4.   .   . G.W.997.

1-20 a.m.   12 large H.E.shell fired over village near
                Fosse No. 7 from direction of AUCHY or HAISNE.   . S.G/67/140th.B.

10-41 a.m.   Attachment of 15th and 16th Lon.Batteries
                to 2nd Division completed.   .   . B.M/763/D.Arty.

6-30 p.m.   LE PHILOSOPHE heavily shelled for 3 hours.
                Bn.H.Qrs., Stores, etc, destroyed.   . S.G.76.

7-20 p.m.   Divl.Res. to be ready to move at 2 hours
                notice.   .   . G.W.6.

21st June (contd).

11-55 p.m.	French firing incendiary shells on LOOS. 5 fires started.	140th Bde. B.M.692/B

VERQUIN. **22nd June, 1915.**

Fine night. Fine morning.

	Germans shelled LES BREBIS with heavy shell, starting about 11-45 p.m. Following casualties in 17th Lon.Bn. - 4 killed, 20 wounded, and 26 suffering from shock.	141st I.Bde. B.M/941 - 2.-4

VERQUIN. **23rd June, 1915.**

Little rain in night. Dull morning.

7-5 pm.	1st Corps Operation Order No. 89, para 3, to be amended - for "Section Y and Z" read "Section Z".	G/918/1st C.

VERQUIN. **24th June, 1915.**

Fine night. Fine morning.

2-5 p.m.	LES BREBIS, N.MAROC, and towards GRENAY being shelled by enemy from direction of LENS.	B.M.999 - 141st S.C.724 - Bde.

VERQUIN. **25th June, 1915.**

Dull night. Wet morning.

8-50 p.m.	1st Div.Hd.Qrs. opens at MARLES LES MINES at 2 p.m. today.	G/456.
11 p.m.	G.O.C. 1st Corps to hold a Conference at Chateau VAUDRICOURT at 3 p.m. 26th June.	G.959/1st C.

VERQUIN. **26th June, 1915.**

Wet night. Fine morning.

	Operation Order No. 10 issued for relief of 140th Inf.Bde. in Section "X" by 142nd Inf.Bde.	Attached.
4-56 p.m.	"W.3" reports being shelled, and also NORTH MAROC, from direction of LENS.	B.M.36/141st B.

VERQUIN. **27th June, 1915.**

Fine night. Fine morning.

10-39 a.m.	Trenches X.1 being shelled with H.E.Shell from direction of AUCHY-LEZ-LA-BASSEE.	S.C.146/140th.
6 p.m.	South MAROC being shelled from direction of LOOS.	S.C.833/141st.

VERQUIN.	**28th June 1915.**	
11-15 a.m.	FOSSE No.7 bombarded by Heavy H.E.Shell from direction of HAISNES.	M.G.150/140th B.
1-20 p.m.	South MAROC shelled.	B.M.96.
4-0 p.m.	Two 15 pdr.batteries attached 2nd Div.will be withdrawn same time as 2nd Div.batteries unless 1st Div.desire to retain them.	G/7/1st C.
4-10 p.m.	PHILOSOPHE being shelled.	S.C.135.
4-47 p.m.	1st Div. desire to retain the two 15 pr batteries for a few days.	G/512/1st Div.
11-59 p.m.	Distribution of 141st Inf.Bde. tonight - 17th Bn. W1, 18th Bn.W2, 19th Bn.W3, 20th Bn.Res.	B.M.106/141st B.

VERQUIN.	**29th June, 1915.**	
	Dull night. Dull morning.	
5-5 a.m.	Relief of 140th Inf.Bde. by 141st Inf.Bde. in Section "X" completed at 12-30 a.m.	G.W.113.
8-18 a.m.	48th Div.H.Q. closes at BUSNES and re-opens at Chateau PHILOMEL, Mensecq, at same hour	G.B.57/48th Div.
12-50 p.m.	G.O.C.4th Corps to hold conference at 2-30 p.m. on 30th at Old Chateau, LA BUISSIERE. G.O.C.,G.S.O.1, and C.R.A's to attend.	G/4718/4th C.
1-10 p.m.	4th Corps assumes command of new front W, X, Y, Z, at 12 noon 30th June.	G/4720/4th C.
1-45 p.m.	1st Corps report centre at LABUISSIERE closes at 3 p.m. and re-opens at Chateau Filette, CHOCQUES at same hour.	G/25/1st C.

VERQUIN.	**30th June 1915.**	
	Wet night and morning.	
10-50 p.m.	2/3rd London Field Co.R.E. less one Section to move to LES BREBIS to be employed under orders of C.R.E.	G/R./132.

W. Ruthven Lieut.Col. /r   Major General,

1st July 1915.   Commanding 47th (London) Division.

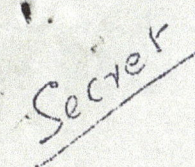

47th (London) Division.

Situation on 3rd June, 1915.

Divisional Headquarters.	VERQUIN Square E.29.b.2.6.
140th Inf.Bde. Headquarters.	NOYELLES-LEZ-VERMELLES.
7th Lon. Regt. Y.1	Firing Line and Supports.
8th do. Y.2	do. do.
6th do.	NOYELLES-LEZ-VERMELLES
15th do.	SAILLY-LABOURSE.
141st Inf. Bde. Headquarters.	Chemist Shop CAMBRIN.
20th Lon. Regt. Y.3	Firing Line and Supports.
17th do. Y.4	do. do.
19th do.	Half at CAMBRIN and half at ANNEQUIN.
18th do. (20th struck through)	ANNEQUIN.
142nd Inf. Bde. Headquarters.	LABOURSE.
21st Lon. Regt.	H.Qrs. & 2 Coys. VERQUIGNEUL 2 Coys. LABOURSE.
22nd do.	LABOURSE.
23rd do.	VERQUIN.
24th do.	VERQUIN.
47th Div. Arty. Headquarters.	Chateau DES PRES.
5th Lon.Bde. R.F.A.	CAMBRIN.
12th Lon.Battry.) in action	F.30.c.2.3
13th do.) do.	F.30.c.4.0
14th do. in reserve	DOUVRIN.
Bde. Ammunition Column.	LE MARAIS.
6th Lon. Bde. R.F.A.	
15th Lon. Battry. in action	G.8.a.9.0
16th do. do.	G.8.c.3.5
17th do. do.	G.8.d.5.5
Bde. Ammunition Column.	L.2.b.4.9
7th Lon.Bde. R.F.A.	L.11.b.
18th Lon. Battry. in reserve	NOYELLES CHATEAU.
19th do. in action	L.6.a.4.8.
20th do. in action	G.7.d.5.5
Bde. Ammunition Column.	K.6.b.9.9
8th Lon. (How.) Bde. R.F.A.	L.11.b.
21st Lon. Battry. in action	G.8.c.3.8
22nd do. do.	G.8.c.5.6
Bde. Ammunition Column.	BEUVRY - F.14.b.2.0
No 8 Trench Mortar Battery	Attached to 141st Infantry Brigade.

Divisional Mounted Troops.
    1 Squadron King Edwards Horse. ⎫
    47th Divisional Cyclist Company. ⎭ . . VAUDRICOURT.

Divisional Engineers.
    3rd London Field Company. . : ⎫
    4th   ,,   ,,   . . : ⎭ SAILLY-LABOURSE.

  4th London Field Ambulance. . . DOUVRIN.
  5th   ,,   ,, . . . LE REVEILLON
  6th   ,,   ,, . . . BETHUNE, ECOLE
                                           MATERNELLE.

47th Divisional Train. . . . HESDIGNEUL.

47th Divisional Ammunition Column. . Woods South of
                                Chateau, DOUVRIN.

47th Divisional Supply Column. . . LOZINGHEM.

                                                                   Lt.Colonel,
                                  W Ruthven
G.R.636.   General Staff
3rd June 1915.   47th (London) Division.

POSITIONS ETC OF 47th DIVISION ARTILLERY

3/6/15.

5th Lon. F.A.B.

    H.Qrs CAMBRIN.
    12th Lon Bty F.30.c.2.5. Wagon line L.2.a.3.5.
    13th : : F.30.c.2.0.   "   "   L.2.a.3.8.
    14th : : In reserve at DROUVIN.
    B.A.C.   LE MARAIS.

6th Lon. F.A.B.

    H.Qrs. NOYELLES-Les-VERMELLES.
    15th Lon Bty.G.8.a.9.0.   Wagon line LA BOURSE.
    16th : : G.8.c.3.3.   :   :   :   :
    17th : : G.8.c.3.2.   :   :   :   :
    B.A.C.   LA BOURSE.

7th Lon F.A.B.

    H.Qrs. NOYELLES- Les-VERMELLES.

    18th Lon.Bty. In reserve at NOYELLES CHATEAU
    19th " : L.6.a.4.8.   Wagon line L.11.b.
    20th : : G.7.d.5.5.   :   :   L.11.b.
    B.A.C.   K.6.b.9.9.

8th Lon(How)F.A.B.

    H.Qrs. NOYELLES-Les-VERMELLES.

    21st Lon Bty.(How) G.8.d.2.4. Wagon line BEUVRY.
    22nd "   "   " G.8.c.7.3.   :   :   :
    B.A.C.   BEUVRY.

47th Div.Amtn. Col. K.9.a and b.

Brigade Major
47th Divisional Artillery.

3/6/15.

47th (London) Division.

TACTICAL PROGRESS REPORT
up to Noon, June 3rd, 1916.

Operations. 1. Nil.

Work. 2. **V.1 Section.**

Fire platforms made and improved. Dug outs made and improved. Lines cleaned and repaired.

L.2 Section.

New fire trench in front of V.2 continued to within 30 yards of Point C. Average depth 3 feet. Saps 12 and 16 cleaned and improved.

L.3 and V.4 Sections.

Cleaning up trenches, improving buttresses and dug-outs, cutting grass.

Information. 3. German working party heard working between Points 1 and 2, Square 11 c. and d., MAICHES Trench Map 2nd Edition. They are probably continuing their fire trench and connecting up T heads to make a fire trench nearer us.

Sounds of digging heard in trench at North West corner of HOHENZOLLERN POST.

Fosse No. 8 used as Observation Post and Snipers' Post.

47th Div. G/61/b   Sgd H.R. Hunt Capt
                       for. Major General,
3rd June, 1916.   Commanding 47th Division.

SECRET.

47TH (LONDON) DIVISION.

Billeting Schedule in reference to G.R. 702 of June 5th 1915.

Divisional Headquarters	VERQUIN.
140th Infantry Brigade	
Headquarters	Chateau, MAZINGARBE
2 Battalions	MAZINGARBE.
1st Line Transport	NOEUX LES MINES.
1 Battn. and 1st Line Transport	NOEUX LES MINES.
1 Battn. attached to 142nd Brigade	LES BREBIS.
1st Line Transport	NOEUX LES MINES.
141st Infantry Brigade.	
Headquarters	LE SAULCHEY FARM L.17.d.
3 Battalions	In Trenches.
1st Line Transport.	HOUCHIN.
1 Battalion.	PHILOSOPHE G.20.a.
1st Line Transport	HOUCHIN
142nd Infantry Brigade.	
Headquarters.	LES BREBIS
4 Battalions	In Trenches
1st Line Transport	HOUCHIN WOOD. K.10.d.
Divisional Mounted Troops.	
C. Squadron, King Edward's Horse.	D.30.c.
Cyclist Company	
Divisional Artillery	
Headquarters	MAZINGARBE.
5th London Brigade	ALLOUAGNE with part LE MARECQUET Wood
B.A.C. less S.A.A. Section	ditto
S.A.A. Section	DROUVIN Wood.
6th London Brigade	S.part of LAPUGNOY with part of BOIS DES DAMES
B.A.C. less 1 Gun Section and S.A.A. Section	ditto
1 Gun Section and S.A.A. Section	DROUVIN Wood.
7th.London Brigade (less 19 Battery).	BELLERY.
B.A.C.	ditto.
19th.Battery in action	R.6a.8.8.
Wagon lines.	DROUVIN Wood.
8th.London(How) Brigade and B.A.C.	FERFAY.
Divnl. Ammunition Column less 1/3rd 15.p.r. Gun portion & S.A.A.Portion.	South Part of LAPUGNOY with part of BOIS DESDAMES.
1/3rd.15.p.r.Gun portion & S.A.A.portion	DROUVIN WOOD.
Divisional Engineers. Headquarters.	MAZINGARBE.
3rd.London Field Company R.E.	LES BREBIS.
4th.London Field Company R.E.	MAZINGARBE.
Divisional Train.	near HESDIGNEUL at D.3.d.
Divisional Supply Column.	ALLOUAGNE.
Medical.	
4th.London Field Ambulance.	Chateau at DROUVIN.
5th.London Field Ambulance.	LE REVELLION.
6th.London Field Ambulance.	NOEUX LES MINES.
with one Section.	LES BREBIS.
and Detachment.	MAZINGARBE.
Sanitary Section.	NOEUX LES MINES.
Motor Ambulance Workshop.	LAPUGNOY.
Convalescent Company.	NOEUX LES MINES.
Mobile Veterinary Section.	DROUVIN.

47th (London) Division.

TACTICAL PROGRESS REPORT,
up to Noon June 9th 1915.

Operations. 1.   Nil.

Work.   2.   W. Section.

                 Improvement of Fire and Communication Trenches.

                 X. Section.

                 Parapet and Communication Trenches repaired.

Information. 3. German front line M.9.d (77) to M.4.a (22) strongly
                 wired, especially at M.4.c (64) where several
                 loopholes are visible.

                 A loopholed trench extends along the North side of
                 the railway embankment running East North East from
                 Puits No. 16. Wire runs along the front of this
                 trench below the embankment from M.10.a (94).

                 A Communication trench runs down the embankment
                 North of M.10.b (03), runs Northwards and appears to
                 join trench at M.4.d (02).

                 A trench runs down the South side of Slag heap at a
                 point about 190 yards South East of M.4.d (97) and
                 joins Communication Trench near M.11.a (19); this
                 trench is protected by wire which runs over the top of
                 the Slag Heap.

                 Communication Trench M.4.b (92) to M.5.a (10) is
                 wired. Wire begins about 200 yards North of M.4.d (97).
                 This trench appears to fork at M.5.a (10). The Eastern
                 branch runs North East to the LENS road at a point
                 about 200 yards South East of G.35.c (34), crosses the
                 road and disappears behind a brushwood screen. It
                 probably joins the trench running to G.35.c (05).

                 Strong double line of wire runs from East end of
                 slag heap M.4 about 100 yards West of M.5.c (82) in an
                 Easterly direction, towards M.5.c (46).

                 Germans were heard putting up wire last night at
                 G.34.c (78) and from G.29.c (71) - G.29.d (03).

                 Wire on line G.29.c (71) to G.29.d (03) is high
                 and broad. There are several gaps about 1 yard
                 wide near the LENS road.

                 The portion of old Communication Trench Sap 13 still
                 in German hands is wired with low wire which runs
                 along North and South sides of branch to the German
                 main line.

47th Div. G/11/3   Major General,

9th June, 1915.   Commanding 47th Division.

Reference Maps.   47th (London) Division.
MAISNES, 2nd Ed.   Tactical Progress Report
and LOOS, 1/10,000.   up to Noon, June 10th 1915.
_____

Operations.   I.   Nil.

Work.   II.   N. Section.
                     Provision of fire steps, blocking loopholes,
               improving parapets and communication trenches.
                     S. Section.
                     Improving trenches. Work of making new front
               line by linking up sapheads continued.

Information. III.   From G.25.c 2.8 to G.28.d (1) is strongly wired.
                     A tunnel appears to run through the German parapet
               at about G.28.b 2.8 into the sap running West South
               West about 200 yards from this point.
                     Dogs were heard barking in the German lines.
                     At G.34.c 8.4 is a short length of trench along the
               North side of the road which looks like a snipers'
               post.
                     South of the road is a large square depression
               surrounded by grass covered mounds. Germans were
               working here on the night of 8th/9th June.
                     During the night of 9th/10th June :-
               (a)   New wire was placed across the Western end of the
                     valley of the Double Crassier and the Germans were
                     working at G.34.a 8.8 and G.28.d 2.8.
                           It is reported that Pipsqueaks are in position
                     in the Crassier.
               (b)   There is a ravine about 100 yards long parallel
                     to the road running South from MAISON LES
                     MITRAILLEURS. This ravine is about 400 yards from
                     our lines. The Germans were working in this
                     ravine during the night.
               (c)   At 7 a.m. 5 men were observed working a wheel at
                     Pit 12.

                                                  H.R. Hunt Capt
               47th Div. G/81/5   /~ Major General,
               10th June, 1915.   Commanding 47th. Division.

Reference Maps.   47th (London) Division.
MAISNIL, 2nd Ed.
and LOOS, 1/10,000.   Tactical Progress Report
                          up to Noon, June 10th 1916.

Operations.   I.   Nil.

Work.   II.   N. Section.
                    Provision of fire stops, blocking loopholes,
                    improving parapets and communication trenches.
                    X. Section.
                    Improving trenches. Work of making new front
                    line by linking up sapheads continued.

Information. III.   From G.28.c 2.6 to G.22.d (1) is strongly wired.
                    A tunnel appears to run through the German parapet
                    at about G.29.b 2.9 into the sap running West South
                    West about 250 yards from this point.
                    Dogs were heard barking in the German lines.
                    At G.24.c 5.4 is a short length of trench along the
                    North side of the road which looks like a snipers'
                    post.
                    South of the road is a large square depression
                    surrounded by grass covered mounds. Germans were
                    working here on the night of 8th/9th June.
                    During the night of 9th/10th June :-
                    (a) New wire was placed across the Western end of the
                        valley of the Double Grassier and the Germans were
                        working at G.34.a 5.5 and G.28.d 2.2.
                        It is reported that Pipsqueaks are in position
                        in the Grassier.
                    (b) There is a ravine about 100 yards long parallel
                        to the road running South from MAISON LES
                        MITRAILLEURS. This ravine is about 400 yards from
                        our lines. The Germans were working in this
                        ravine during the night.
                    (c) At 7 a.m. 5 men were observed working a wheel at
                        Pit 14.

                                              H.R. Hunt Capt
47th Div. G/21/6   for Major General,
10th June, 1916.   Commanding 47th. Division.

47th (LONDON) DIVISION.

WAR DIARY - GENERAL STAFF

JUNE, 1915.

BETHUNE.   1st June 1915.

Fine night. Fine morning.

1-55 a.m.	6th London Battalion reported relieved by 20th Brigade. 15th Lon.Battn. relieved by Grenadier Guards. 140th Inf.Bde. H.Q. open at 8 Boulevarde Frederick De Georges, BETHUNE.	B.M.36. B.M.37.
7-30 a.m.	2nd Canadian Brigade will begin to relieve right Brigade of 47th (London) Division at 4-40 p.m. today.	G/655/Can.Div.
10-30 a.m.	1st Corps Hd.Qrs. closes at CHOCQUES at 3 p.m. today and opens at Chateau, LA BUISSIERE (J.4.c.8.2.) at same hour.	G/623/1st C.
	140th Inf.Bde. Sig. Sec. to relieve 1st Guards Bde. Sig. Sec. as soon as possible. G.O.C. 1st Guards Bde. to remain in his present H.Q. in command of sub-section until relieved by 141st Inf.Bde. Whole section under command of G.O.C. 1st Div. till 6 p.m. 2nd June. 1st Gds.Bde. can call on 140th Inf.Bde. if necessary.	G.H.613.
11-50 a.m.	Lt.Col. W. Thwaites, R.A. to command 141st Inf.Bde. Lt.Col. The Hon. W.P. Hore-Ruthven, C.M.G., D.S.O., to be G.S.O. 1st Grade, 47th Division.	A.Q.596.
2-55 p.m.	47th Division to take over command of "Y" and "Z" Sections from 6 p.m. 2nd June.	
3-30 p.m.	140th Inf.Bde. to take over whole of Section "Y" from 6 p.m. this evening. This will include Y.3 and Y.4 now held by 2 battalions of 1st Division.	G/190/1st Div.
3-50 p.m.	Situation of Artillery Headquarters and units.	B.M/83.
4-20 p.m.	Headquarters 141st Inf.Bde. open at 8 Boulevarde Frederick De Georges, BETHUNE, at 7-30 p.m. tonight.	B.M.510.
9-0 p.m.	Adv. 2nd Div. Hd.Qrs. open at Chateau MAZINGARBE at 9 a.m. 2nd June. 2nd Div.Hd.Qrs. remain at Chateau LEZ CHARMEUX.	G/893/2nd Div.
	140th Inf.Bde. Hd.Qrs. opened at NOYELLES LEZ VERMELLES at 7 p.m. today.	B.M.47.

2.

BETHUNE.	2nd June 1915.	

Fine night - Fine morning.

1-20 a.m.   Reliefs in Y.1 and Y.2 completed.   B.M/120/140th B.

3-14 p.m.   141st Inf.Bde.H.Q. moves from BETHUNE and will open at CAMBRIN at 5-30 p.m.   B.M.529.

3-40 p.m.   142nd Inf.Bde. report situation of units.   B.M.703.

4-0 p.m.   47th Div.Hd.Qrs. closes at Level Crossing (E.4.a.7.5.) at 4 p.m. and re-opens at same hour at VERQUIN (E.29.b.2.6.).   G.H.626.

6-15 p.m.   G.O.C. 1st Division hands over command of "Y" and "Z" Sections to G.O.C. 47th Division.   G/208/1st Div.

3rd June 1915.

VERQUIN.   Nothing happened. Z.1.Section renumbered Y.4.

Situation of units.   Attached.

VERQUIN.   4th June 1915.

Fine night - dull misty morning.

5-30 a.m.   Quiet night reported.

9-35 a.m.   7th Divn. captured I.2 and I.4 last night but were bombed out this morning.   (Telephone).

7-50 p.m.   Preliminary order for relief of 2nd Divn. issued to formations of 47th Div. (Secret).

8-45 p.m.   2nd Divn. to take over 47th Div. line. Detailed orders later.

VERQUIN.   5th June 1915.

Fine night. Fine hot morning.

5-30 a.m.   Quiet night reported.

12-35 p.m.   1st Corps call for programme of reliefs according to 1st Corps Operation Order 88.   G.R.696.
Sent 2-12 p.m.   G.676/1st C.

2-45 p.m.   Received Time Table for movements of 2nd Div.Troops through NOEUX LES MINES.   G.943/2nd Div.

6-0 p.m.   140th Inf.Bde.ordered, on relief by 6th Bde., to send one battalion to LES BREBIS to come under orders of 142nd Inf.Bde.   G.W.700.

9-25 p.m.   One battn. 141st Inf.Bde. to move into LES BREBIS night 6th/7th to be at disposal of 142nd Inf.Bde. till night 7th/8th.   G.W.706.

3.

VERQUIN.	**6th June 1915.**	

Fine night. Fine morning.

Quiet night reported.

7-55 a.m.	142nd Inf.Bde. informed that road through NOEUX LES MINES available between 9-30 and 10-30 p.m. and not as stated in G.R. 703.	G.W.715.
10-0 a.m.	Command of sub-sections to pass to G.O.C's relieving Bde. as soon as reliefs are completed.	G.H.716.
11-5 a.m.	200 spades and 150 picks to be kept in "W" and "X" Sections.	G.H.719.
1-0 p.m.	2nd Div. propose that their C.R.A. should take over Y.1 - Y.4 from 6 p.m. June 7th. C.R.A. 47th Div. proposed to take over 2nd Div. Section Artillery same date.	B.M.241.
5-0 p.m.	Alteration in Operation Orders G.R.702	G.W.724.

VERQUIN.	**7th June 1915.**	

Fine night. Fine morning - very hot.

1-25 a.m.	Relief of 141st Bde. in Y.3 and Y.4 completed.	G.W.732.
2-0 a.m.	Reliefs in Section "W" reported complete.	G.W.733.
5-30 a.m.	Quiet night, except for intermittent M.G.Fire.	
11-35 a.m.	All Inf.Bdes. told they can draw S.A.A. from any of the F.A.Bdes.Ammn.Cols.at DROUVIN WOOD.	G.R.741.
6-0 p.m.	Adv.2nd Div. closed at MAZINGARBE and reopened at Chateau DES PRES at 6 p.m.	G.987/2nd Div.
6-45 p.m.	All ranks forbidden to approach batteries in action. No officers to enter artillery Observation Posts without permits from G.S.	G.H.754.
7-45 p.m.	Both batteries of Howitzers can be withdrawn to reserve.	G.R.755.
8-0 p.m.	1st Corps ask that any heavy artillery bombardment should be reported.	G.H.757.
8-35 p.m.	141st Inf.Bde.H.Q. moving to LE SAULCHY FM (L.17.d) Established at 10 p.m.	B.M.655.
10-30 p.m.	Germans seen near A.2, apparently experimenting with poisonous gases.	G.H.760.

VERQUIN.	**8th June 1915.**	

Fine night. Fine morning.

1-30 a.m.	Reliefs complete in Section X and command of section taken over by 141st Inf.Bde.	G.H.763.
	Much wheeled traffic heard moving South from opposite L.8.	G.H.764.

8th June (contd).

1-45 a.m.	140th Inf.Bde.H.Q. opens at MAZINGARBE. Reliefs complete.	B.M.78.
8-0 a.m.	1st Corps orders arrangements to be made for co-operation of two 4.7 batteries with French XXI Corps on right. Wireless being placed at our disposal for this purpose.	G.713/1st C.
10-0 a.m.	1st Corps report that asphyxiating gas pressure pump has arrived at ILLIES. Sharp look-out to be kept.	G.714/1st C.
10-10 a.m.	1st Corps order gas proof M.G.Emplacement to be made early.	G.716/1st C.
12 noon to 12-30 p.m.	Enemy shelled North of Sub-Secn.X.2. Strong line of wire from M.11.a.19. to M.10.a.94. Enemy's line strongly wired from M.4.a.22 to G.34.c.78, especially near latter.	

VERQUIN.

9th June 1915.

Fine night. Fine morning. Thunder and rain during afternoon of 8th.

8-20 a.m.	140th Inf.Bde. report reserve M.G.Teams in all battalions.	M.G.92.

VERQUIN.

10th June 1915.

Fine night. Dull morning.

10-40 a.m.	Only traffic allowed on road running from Chateau MAZINGARBE to LE SAULCHOY FARM is that proceeding to Hd.Qrs.47th Div.Engrs., and French Arty.Comdrs.Hd.Qrs. No troops to drill in field S.E. of the road.	G.R.801.
11-55 a.m.	R.E. ordered to supply about 30 short scaling ladders for 142nd Inf.Bde.	G.R.803.

VERQUIN.

11th June 1915.

Rain during night. Dull morning.

6-45 a.m.	1st Corps call conference of G.O's.C. 1st, 2nd and 47th Divisions at VAUDRICOURT at 11 a.m. C.R.A's and G.S.O's to attend.	G.H.817.
	Enemy shelled sub-section X.1 during day.	

VERQUIN.

12th June 1915.

Fine night. Dull morning.

5-15 a.m.	Large german working party fired on opposite X.2., by 141st Inf.Bde.	B.M.758.
	Number of days in and out of trenches received from Inf.Bdes. List attached.	

12th June (contd).

	140th Inf.Bde. relieve 141st Inf.Bde. tonight, in Section "X".	G.H.831 of 11th.
	15th Lon.Battn. to remain with 142nd Inf. Bde. One battalion of 141st Inf.Bde. to be at disposal of 140th Bde. (battn.at PHILOSOPHE).	
3-5 p.m.	On relief tonight, 141st Inf.Bde. H.Q. will be at NOEUX LES MINES.	
	140th Inf.Bde.H.Q. remain at MAZINGARBE Chateau.	G.R.845.
10-10 p.m.	Battalions in Divisional Reserve to be ready to move at 2 hours notice.	G.R.859.
7-55 p.m.	German observation balloon up and able to see down street where reserve companies of X.1 and X.2 are billeted. It will be fired on tomorrow if within 10,000 yards.	B.M.783.
11-32 p.m.	Relief of 141st Inf.Bde. by 140th Inf.Bde. completed at 10-40 p.m.	S.C.339.

VERQUIN.   ## 13th June 1915.

Fine night.   Fine morning.

7-59 a.m.	Situation of units of 140th Inf.Bde.:- 6th Bn. X.1., 7th Bn. X.2., 8th Bn.PHILOSOPHE. 15th Bn(attached) - half PHILOSOPHE and half at MAZINGARBE.	B.M.127.
8-15 a.m.	Situation of units of 141st Inf.Bde. 19th and 20th Lon.Bns. at MAZINGARBE; 18th Bn. at NOEUX LES MINES. Bde.Hd.Qrs.- LE SAULCHOY FM.	B.M.791.
9-6 a.m.	142nd Inf.Bde. units disposed as follows :- 21st Bn. in W.1., ~~22nd Bn.~~ 15th Bn. W.2., 23rd Bn. & 1 Coy.24th Bn. W.3., 22nd Bn. and remainder of 24th Bn. in Bde.Reserve at LES BREBIS.	B.M.760.
7-25 p.m.	141st Inf.Bde.H.Q. established at NOEUX LES MINES (K.18.b.4.3.).	B.M.801.
	During day enemy used trench mortars against W.1 and W.3.	
	Constant stream of traffic heard from 9-0 to 11-30 p.m. moving South from LOOS.	

VERQUIN.   ## 14th June 1915.

Fine night.   Fine day - cooler.

9-30 a.m.	When 15th Lon.Bn. is relieved from trenches on night 16th/17th, it will rejoin 140th Inf.Bde. and its place will be taken by a battn. of the 141st Inf.Bde.	G.R.887.
5-10 p.m.	Lieut.GAUTERON does not think Germans were mining or likely to mine under 142nd Inf.Bde.Area.	G.H.894.
8-45 p.m.	113th Batty.R.G.A. at disposal of 2nd Divn. not 47th Div.	'Phone.

14th June (contd).

11-50 p.m.   Bombing party of 15th Lon.Bn. attacked SNIPERS HOUSE. One German look-out man ran back. Germans manned their trenches. No casualties to our men.   ('phone).

VERQUIN.   ## 15th June, 1915.

Fine night. Fine morning - warmer.

10-0 a.m.   Bombing attack on German Sap opposite Sap 18. The attack started at 10-30 p.m. and had the effect of rousing the Germans who opened heavy rifle and shell fire and clearly had a large number of men in trenches. Sap destroyed in some places by enemy's shell fire. Sap obviously registered. No casualties.   B/645.

Report of Trench Mortar attack on Sap 12. Commenced at 10-30 p.m. Average of 9 rounds per Mortar fired in 15 minutes. Very little response except a little Machine Gun Fire. Sap apparently hit; also salient of German trench opposite left of battery.

12-40 p.m.   Certain amount of movement around LILLE, DON, etc. Probably reinforcements for NEUVE CHAPELLE Section. Unlikely to be more than one regiment.   G/793/1st C.

3-40 p.m.   142nd Inf.Bde.asked to consider and give an opinion on desirability of joining our line near Sap 18 with MAISON DES MITRAILLEURS, thus reducing length of line. Also asked for estimate of work required.   G.R/905.

5-37 p.m.   Scaling ladders and bayonets displayed in X.1. Enemy opened heavy shrapnel fire on X.1 and communication trenches. French Artillery replied effectively.   G.H/908.

8-0 p.m.   Message to Colonel Muller and French Artillery thanking them for work done in co-operation with 47th Division.   G.R/911.

8-10 p.m.   Observation Officer's report. Canadians have taken H.4,-H.15. 7th Div. captured first line and working up towards 2nd Line. 51st Division have reached N corner of RUE D'OUVERT and are bombing down it (not yet officially confirmed). Up till then no intense bombardment on our troops. 1st Corps attribute this to operations of 47th Division.   Confirmed 8-45 p.m.   G.H.912. G/797/1st C.

10-20 p.m.   140th Inf.Bde. report German scaling ladders distinctly seen opposite Sap 16. Great vigilance ordered.   S.C.518.

VERQUIN.   ## 16th June, 1915.

Fine night. Fine morning.

7-5 a.m.   Heavy bombing counter-attack compelled our troops to withdraw from positions gained last night North of Canal.   G/801/1st C.

16th June (contd).

9-35 a.m.	Detailed account of above from 1st Corps. 2nd Army report having penetrated German lines in several points from HOOGE CHATEAU - YPRES - ROULERS Ry.	G/802/1st C.
5-25 p.m.	1st Corps order that no reliefs are to take place tonight.	G.H/924.
6-25 p.m.	French reported to have captured front line of German trenches. French troops have reached ridge S.E. of SOUCHEZ.	G/808/1st C.
7-0 p.m.	4th Corps occupied L.10 and I.2 - I.4.	
7-20 p.m.	2nd Army report not much progress. German counter-attack failed.	G/413/1st C.
9-42 p.m.	141st Inf.Bde.H.Q. established at MAZINGARBE.	B.M.860.
10-40 p.m.	4th Corps have taken L.10 - L.8 - K.6 - J.10 and I.2 - I.4. Driven out of all except K.6 - J.10.	G/818/1st C.

VERQUIN.

17th June 1915.

Fine night. Fine day.

8-50 a.m.	6th Inf.Bde. no longer in Corps Reserve. 1st Guards Brigade remain in Corps Reserve.	G/823/1st C.
10-10 a.m.	Reliefs which were postponed last night may be carried out tonight.	G.H.937.
11-0 a.m.	141st Inf.Bde. will relieve 142nd Inf.Bde. in Section "W" on night 20th/21st June. 142nd Inf. Bde. will billet 2 battns at MAZINGARBE, remainder at NOEUX LES MINES.	G.H.938.
12-27 p.m.	Amendments to 142nd Bde.Operation Order No.22, received.	B.M.792
1-9 p.m.	141st Inf.Bde.H.Q. established at NOEUX LES MINES	B.M.868.
2-45 p.m.	Major Hermon, K.E.H., to take over charge of Divl.Bombing School, with effect from 18th June.	G.H.941.
3-9 p.m.	Battalions of 141st Inf.Bde. usually billeted at NOEUX LES MINES will remain for the present at MAZINGARBE. Working parties from brigades for tonight to be detailed as usuals.	G.H.940.
6-40 p.m.	$1\frac{1}{2}$ in Trench Mortar Battery sent to 140th Inf. Bde. for "X" Section. 95 mm Trench Mortars now in "X" to be transferred to "W" Section.	G.H.946.
8-10 p.m.	$1\frac{1}{2}$ in T.M.Battery will reach 140th Bde. in morning instead of tinight as at first ordered.	G.H.948.
10-20 p.m.	Railway activity about LENS. All precautions to be taken against hostile attack.	G/831/1st C.

VERQUIN.   18th June 1915.

                Fine night. Fine day.

8-59 a.m.   In event of hostile attack, working parties will not attempt to rejoin their own units during the attack unless they are working close to battn assembly place. They will attach themselves to the nearest unit. . . G.H.957.

5-55 p.m.   When reporting gun flashes at night, exact time should be stated. . . I.G/48/1st C.

VERQUIN.   19th June 1915.

                Fine night. Fine morning.

8-45 a.m.   1st Corps report unusual railway activity at LA BASSEE and DON about 4 - 5 a.m. . G/849/1st C.

4-15 p.m.   Two 15 pr Batteries of 47th Div. will move into position night 20th/21st June and will be attached to 2nd Division. . G/852/1st C.

9-0 p.m.   G.O.C. held conference of Brigadiers at MAZINGARBE at 9 p.m.

10-15 p.m.   Relief of "W" Section arranged for night of 20th/21st is postponed till night 21st/22nd. G.H.983.

                        20th June 1915.

                Fine night. Fine morning.

1-0 p.m.   G.O.C. orders conference of G.O.C., R.A., C.R.E., and Inf.Brigadiers, at MAZINGARBE Chateau at 4 p.m. today. . . G.H.986.

6-0 p.m.   Relief of 142nd Inf.Bde. by 141st Inf.Bde. to be carried out tonight as originally ordered. G.W.991.

6-35 p.m.   Squadron K.E.H. to do 48 hours in trenches attached 141st Inf.Bde. . . H.H.992.

                        21st June 1915.

VERQUIN,   Fine night. Fine morning.

1-0 a.m.   Relief of "W" Section completed. Command of Section taken over by 141st Bde. W.1 - 18th Bn. W.2 - 20th Bn., W.3 - 19th Bn. Bde.Res.- 17th Bn. Bde.H.Qrs. at K.18.c.3.4. . G.W.997.

1-20 a.m.   12 large H.E. shell fired over village near Fosse No. 7 from direction of AUCHY or HAISNE. . S.C/67/140th.B.

10-41 a.m. Attachment of 15th and 16th Lon.Batteries to 2nd Division completed. . B.M/763/D.Arty.

6-30 p.m.   LE PHILOSOPHE heavily shelled for 3 hours. Bn.H.Qrs., Stores, etc, destroyed. . S.C.76.

7-20 p.m.   Divl.Res. to be ready to move at 2 hours notice. . . G.W.6.

21st June (contd).

11-55 p.m.	French firing incendiary shells on LOOS. 5 fires started.	140th Bde. B.M.692/B

VERQUIN. **22nd June, 1915.**

Fine night. Fine morning.

	Germans shelled LES BREBIS with heavy shell, starting about 11-45 p.m. Following casualties in 17th Lon.Bn. - 4 killed, 20 wounded, and 26 suffering from shock.	141st I.Bde. B.M/941 - 2.

VERQUIN. **23rd June, 1915.**

Little rain in night. Dull morning.

7-5 pm.	1st Corps Operation Order No. 89, para 3, to be amended - for "Section Y and Z", read "Section "Z".	G/918/1st C.

VERQUIN. **24th June, 1915.**

Fine night. Fine morning.

2-5 p.m.	LES BREBIS, N.MAROC, and towards GRENAY being shelled by enemy from direction of LENS.	B.M.999 - 141st S.C.724 - Bde.

VERQUIN. **25th June, 1915.**

Dull night. Wet morning.

8-50 p.m.	1st Div.Hd.Qrs. opens at MARLES LES MINES at 2 p.m. today.	G/456.
11 p.m.	G.O.C. 1st Corps to hold a Conference at Chateau VAUDRICOURT at 3 p.m. 26th June.	G.959/1st C.

VERQUIN. **26th June, 1915.**

Wet night. Fine morning.

	Operation Order No. 10 issued for relief of 140th Inf.Bde. in Section "X" by 142nd Inf.Bde.	Attached.
4-58 p.m.	"W.3" reports being shelled, and also NORTH MAROC, from direction of LENS.	B.M.36/141st B.

VERQUIN. **27th June, 1915.**

Fine night. Fine morning.

10-39 a.m.	Trenches X.1 being shelled with H.E.Shell from direction of AUCHY-LEZ-LA-BASSEE.	S.C.146/140th.
6 p.m.	South MAROC being shelled from direction of LOOS.	S.C.833/141st.

VERQUIN.   28th June 1915.

11-15 a.m.   FOSSE No.7 bombarded by Heavy H.E.Shell
                  from direction of HAISNES.   .   .   M.G.150/140th B.

1-20 p.m.   South MAROC shelled.   .   .   B.M.96.

4-0 p.m.   Two 15 pdr.batteries attached 2nd Div.will
                  be withdrawn same time as 2nd Div.batteries unless
                  1st Div.desire to retain them.   .   .   G/7/1st C.

4-10 p.m.   PHILOSOPHE being shelled.   .   .   S.C.135.

4-47 p.m.   1st Div. desire to retain the two 15 pr batteries
                  for a few days.   .   .   G/512/1st Div.

11-59 p.m.   Distribution of 141st Inf.Bde. tonight -
                  17th Bn. W1, 18th Bn.W2, 19th Bn.W3, 20th Bn.Res. B.M.106/141st B.

VERQUIN.   29th June, 1915.

                  Dull night.   Dull morning.

5-5 a.m.   Relief of 140th Inf.Bde. by 141st Inf.Bde. in
                  Section "X" completed at 12-30 a.m.   .   G.W.113.

8-18 a.m.   48th Div.H.Q. closes at BUSNES and re-opens
                  at Chateau PHILOMEL, Mensecq, at same hour   .   G.B.57/48th Div.

12-50 p.m.   G.O.C.4th Corps to hold conference at 2-30
                  p.m. on 30th at Old Chateau, LA BUISSIERE.
                  G.O.C.,G.S.O.1, and C.R.A's to attend.   .   G/4718/4th C.

1-10 p.m.   4th Corps assumes command of new front W, X,
                  Y, Z, at 12 noon 30th June.   .   .   G/4720/4th C.

1-45 p.m.   1st Corps report centre at LABUISSIERE closes
                  at 3 p.m. and re-opens at Chateau Filette,
                  CHOCQUES at same hour.   .   .   G/25/1st C.

VERQUIN.   30th June 1915.

                  Wet night and morning.

10-30 p.m.   2/3rd London Field Co.R.E. less one Section
                  to move to LES BREBIS to be employed under
                  orders of C.R.E.   .   .   G/R./132.

                                    W. Ruthven Lieut. Col. for Major General,
         1st July 1915.   Commanding 47th (London) Division.

"F" CG/216 June 1915

DEFENCE SCHEME
"W" and "X" Sections.

1. The Sector now held by the 47th Division extends from the GRENAY - LENS Road (inclusive) on the South to the LE RUTOIRE - LOOS Road (inclusive).

   It is divided into two Sections "W" and "X".

   "W" Section extends from the GRENAY - LENS Road (inclusive) to the MAZINGARBE - LENS Road (exclusive).

   "X" Section extends from the MAZINGARBE - LENS Road (inclusive) to the LE RUTOIRE - LOOS Road (inclusive).

2. The general arrangements for the defence of this line will be as follows :-

   (i) The "A" Line will be held at all costs.

   (ii) The troops in "B" Line are the supports of the "A" Line and will be employed for immediate counterstroke in case the enemy breaks into the "A" Line.

   (iii) The garrison of the Keeps in "C" Line will be found by the Troops in Brigade Reserve.
   Each Keep, as soon as completed, will be permanently garrisoned by one Section, with a Machine Gun, and arrangements will be made to send up immediately the remainder of the Platoon to each Keep in the event of an attack.

   (iv) Troops in Brigade Reserve, less the garrison of Keeps in "C" Line, will be employed to make any further counterstrokes necessary under the orders of the Brigadier.

   (v) Troops in Divisional Reserve, consisting of the Infantry Brigade not holding a Section of the Defensive Line and the Divisional Mounted Troops, will be employed for counter attacks and for securing the Advanced Second Line under the orders of the Divisional Commander. They will normally be ready to move at two hours notice.

3. A tracing showing the position of the Artillery of the Division in support of the Sector is attached.

4. On receipt of orders to move, the G.O.C. Infantry Brigade in Divisional Reserve will at once move to his Advanced Headquarters at MAZINGARBE at the same time sending an Officer to report to Divisional Report Centre at NOEUX LES MINES.

The O.C. Divisional Mounted Troops will send a Mounted Officer with two Cyclist Orderlies to report at the Divisional Report Centre.

The Infantry Brigade in Divisional Reserve and the Divisional Mounted Troops will assemble in one of the alternative positions already reconnoitred immediately in rear of MAZINGARBE or LES BREBIS according to the direction in which its action is likely to be developed.

This action may be :-

(a) In support of the French Infantry Brigade immediately on the right of the British Line. This support would most probably be afforded as the result of a compulsory retirement of this French Brigade from their first line to the continuation, on the French side, of the GRENAY Line of Defence, and would, normally, take the form of a counter-attack against the flank of the advancing enemy in the direction of the "Arbre de Conde", i.e., over the open ground South of GRENAY and East of BULLY-GRENAY.

In this contingency, it will be desirable for the G.O.C. Infantry Brigade in Divisional Reserve to retain one Battalion in Brigade Reserve to meet eventualities, or, if there is a likelihood of our line in "W" being forced, to garrison the GRENAY Line of Defence in the part most threatened. This reserve battalion may also be required for direct counter-attack in support of our own first line about the "MAROC."

(b) In case of attack in strength by the enemy against "W"1 and "W"2, i.e., against the "MAROC."

In this case the Infantry Brigade in Divisional Reserve will concentrate in rear of LES BREBIS. Its action will be essentially offensive, but the Brigadier should, as in (a) maintain a reserve under his own hand, and will be responsible for the safety of the GRENAY Line of Defence, on the front threatened, until its garrison is relieved by Corps Reserves.

It may be assumed that in the eventuality of the British First Line being forced in this Section that the French will assist by a counter-attack delivered across the British front, in which case it will be endeavoured to make the counter-attack of the Infantry Brigade in Divisional Reserve coincide with the French movement.

(c) Against German attack North of the "MAROC" the Infantry Brigade in Divisional Reserve will assemble in rear of MAZINGARBE. As in the other eventualities its action must be in the first place offensive, but it is necessary that the GRENAY - VERMELLES Line should be secured against a coup-de-main until Corps Reserves are available to release its garrison.

It should be remembered, in connection with the employment of the Divisional Reserve in "X" Section, that the expediency may arise of supporting, under Corps instructions, the division on the left, by action in front of VERMELLES.

Commanders of all Infantry Brigades, C.Os., Adjutants and Company Commanders of battalions, the Senior Officers of the Divisional Mounted Troops and Field Companies are responsible that all ground, both French and English, as well as the approaches to it, are thoroughly reconnoitred previously. The C.R.A. will, in like manner, carefully prepare his artillery support for cooperation in offense and defense.

47th Div

R.W. 12   9th June.

With a view to assisting the operations of 4th Corps North of the Canal, which are to take place on 12th June, please submit proposals for diverting the enemy's attention by wire cutting, digging, and any suitable minor enterprise in 47th Div area.

It is not intended that an infantry attack of any importance is to be made by the troops under your command

A copy of 4th Corps Operation Order 24 is being forwarded for your information. This order prescribed the 9th–11th June as the dates for the operations N. of Canal. They have now been postponed 48 hrs

1st Corps 12-15 pm   Rawlinson KGPS

1st Army No. 238 (G).

G/226

First Army.

In order to assist other formations who may be called upon to undertake similar tasks, will you kindly forward any notes you may have which brings out the difficulties experienced in the recent operations of your Army and the measures taken to cope with them.

Information is specially required on :-

(a) Communications after the infantry have advanced.

(b) How hostile machine guns were dealt with.

(c) Methods taken to indicate positions reached by our own troops.

Any other points of interest will be of value.

The notes can be quite rough as they will be edited for issue at G.H.Q.

G.S. H.H.Q.   Sd. E.M. Perceval. Brig. General.
  9th June, 1915.   Sub-Chief, General Staff.

(2).

1st Corps.

Please furnish any such notes by Sunday evening, the 13th instant.

         Sd. R. Butler. Brig. General.
10th June, 1915.   General Staff, 1st Army.

(3).

~~1st Division.~~
~~2nd Division.~~
47th Division.

Please forward any notes you may have by 9am 13th June

         Brig. General.
11th June, 1915.   General Staff, 1st Corps.

1st Corps.

Reference 1st Army 238/G forwarded by you on 10th instant, the following notes have been made :-

(a) Telephones and wire should go over with the first party after the assault.

The wires however were constantly being broken and telephones could not be depended upon.

Most of the communication was done by runners and it is rather a matter of luck whether they get through or not. Each runner before starting should know exactly where to go, and should lay out a light telephone wire as he runs; a runner or even two being sent off as soon as a break occurs, thus not only carrying a message but also attempting to re-establish telephonic communication.

Signalling with electric lamps can be usefully employed on a dull day, but it is useless on a sunny day.

It is essential also at once (after dark) to run out a communication trench to the forward line, so as to get wounded back; and ammunition, bombs, rations and water up. The quickest method is to run out a line of canvas screen, and to dig a trench alongside, using the earth from it to bank up the canvas. If there is not time to finish the trench, the screen gives cover from view, which is much better than nothing.

(b) Possible machine gun positions were located before the attack. They were engaged by the Artillery and also by Trench Mortars and rifle grenades.

14 Trench Mortars of different sorts engaged suspected Machine Gun Positions from I.4 to H.3. It is known that there were several Machine Guns between these two points and it is believed that they could not come into action at all.

It is suggested that REXER or LEWIS rifles with telescopic sights be issued for the purpose of engaging Machine Guns. These rifles could be easily taken forward in the advance and brought into action rapidly. They would also be useful for covering fire during double blocking, especially in a place like the CLIFF at I.4 where there was only room for one or two men at a time.

(c) The method of marking the positions reached by our own troops by means of flags or discs now in use, is satisfactory. Flags are preferable to discs. Complaints have been made that the discs in use with this Division are too heavy. The French have a light pattern consisting of a wire frame with a red cotton material stretched over it. This they planted on the parapet by means of a spike attachment. One man can easily carry ten to a dozen of these discs.

(d) Infantry Observing Officers posted in our trenches gave continuous and accurate information of the progress of operations, as did the Artillery Observations Officers.

/(e)

(e) The enemy's wire should be destroyed as early as possible on each side of the gap already made so as to admit of a broader front over which to reinforce to counter attack should he recapture a portion of his original line.

(f) As many communication trenches as possible from front to rear should be made in our lines before the attack. These should be told off as "up" and "down" routes, and picketed to ensure that they are used for traffic in one direction only. If this is not possible numerous sidings and crossing places should be made.
Though it may sound brutal the evacuation of wounded must not commence until some two or three hours after the assault has been delivered, otherwise the communication trenches become congested and men carrying stores and tools give way to stretcher bearers bringing down the wounded.

(g) The great mistake has always been that our artillery cease fire after the position is taken. They should go on shelling the whole surrounding country and all possible gun positions, for at least another 24 to 48 hours so as to give full time for the position to be consolidated, everybody properly dug in, and efficient communication trenches made where necessary.

(h) A copy of Notes sent in by 142nd Infantry Brigade immediately after the attack of that Brigade, is attached. The last note re dulling of bayonets is of importance.

47th Div. G/226

13th June, 1915.

W. Ruthven Lt. Col. /r Major General,
Commanding 47th (London) Division.

APPENDIX.

NOTES by 142nd Infantry Brigade.

Captain MILNER, 24th Battalion, informed me after the operations that the enemy suffered considerable casualties in their counter-attacks on the captured trench.

Communication Trenches. Only two of these were available for traffic to and from the support trench NEW CUT, and proved insufficient for the passage of working parties and the evacuation of the wounded.

Sidings and frequent passing places are required in all communication trenches, which should be well traversed and as roomy as possible.

Packs though empty, and haversacks, were found to catch considerably in the trenches and delay progress.

A method of carrying wounded men out of the trenches, which is necessary if free communication is to be maintained, requires to be organised.

A method of carrying water up to front line trenches is required.

Efficient working of trench mortar and rifle grenades is of the greatest assistance in bombing down a trench which can be brought under flank fire from our own trenches.

I am of the opinion that Rexer Rifles would be of great assistance in consolidating a trench whence an important field of fire can only be obtained from a constricted fire position.

Company officers report that the bayonets flashing in the sun gave away the advance directly our men mounted the parapet to assault.

Some method of dulling or browning these appears to be very necessary during the bright summer months.

SECRET.

Copy No. 5.

4)Div G/227

OPERATION ORDER No. 24
by
LIEUT. GENERAL SIR H.S. RAWLINSON, BART., K.C.B., C.V.O.,
Commanding IVth Army Corps.

Headquarters IVth Corps.
7th June, 1915.

1. With the object of gaining ground in the direction of VIOLAINES, the IVth Corps will attack and capture the German positions along the RUE D'OUVERT from L.12 on the north via CHAPELLE ST. ROCH - I.17 - I.15, to the British trench line south of H.2. The 51st Division will attack the northern end of the RUE D'OUVERT, the 7th Division the southern end and CHAPELLE ST. ROCH, whilst the Canadian Division will form a defensive flank I.17 - I.16 - H.2.

2. The 51st (Highland) Division.
The objective of the 51st (Highland) Division will be the houses at L.12, L.11, L.13 and K.7, at which latter point they will join hands with the 7th Division.
The division will attack the enemy's salient opposite L.8, and after gaining possession of the line L.9 - L.10, will press on rapidly to L.11, L.12, L.13.
The German trench line about K.7 and L.9, as well as the houses at J.15 and J.12 will be kept under heavy artillery and small arm fire up to the moment that the assault is launched, and this fire will be maintained on K.7 and J.15 during and after the assault.

3. The 7th Division.
The attack of the 7th Division will be directed against J.15 - J.16 - I.11, with the ultimate objective K.8 - CHAPELLE ST. ROCH - I.18. The division will break in on the front I.4 - I.7 and, having gained possession of the trenches as far as J.16 - I.11, will attack the house at J.15 from the south, and then press forward against J.18, J.20, and J.12.

4. Canadian Division.
The Canadian Division will break through the enemy's line on the front H.3 - H.2 (both inclusive) and will establish a protective flank on the line I.17 - I.16 to H.2, joining up with their present line 200 yards south of H.2.

5. The attacks of the 7th, 51st, and Canadian Divisions will be delivered simultaneously at the conclusion of the artillery bombardment, a detailed time-table of which will be issued. The infantry attack will be delivered on the morning of June 11th and will be preceded by a deliberate artillery bombardment lasting 48 hours and becoming intense immediately before the infantry assault is launched. The hour at which the assault will be made will be notified later.

6. Artillery.
The whole of the Divisional and attached artillery will be under the command of Brigadier-General J.F.N. Birch, A.D.C. In addition to the bombardment of the enemy's positions and the establishment of barrages of fire, wire will be cut as follows :-
   (a) In front of 51st Division.
       At L.9, L.10, opposite L.8, and half way between M.10 and L.12.
   (b) In front of the 7th Division.
       On the front I.4, I.2, I.7.
   (c) In front of the Canadian Division.
       On the front H.3 - H.2.

7. The Divisional and attached artillery will be grouped as follows :-

Highland Division.	(Brig.Gen. H.A. Brendon).	Guns.
18 prs.	9th Bde. R.F.A. (19, 20, 28).	18
15 prs.	1st and 2nd Highland Bdes.	24
5" Hows.	3rd Highland Brigade.	8
75 mm.	French.	7

Nicholson Group.	(Lt. Col. Nicholson).	
18 prs.	35th Bde. R.F.A. (12, 25, 58).	18
18 prs.	1st Canadian Bde. (1, 2, 3, 4).	16

Alexander Group.	(Lt. Col. Alexander, V.C.)	
18 prs.	22nd Bde. R.F.A. (104, 105, 106).	18
75 mm.	French.	9

Canadian Group.	(Brig. Gen. Burstall).	
18 prs.	2nd Canadian Bde. (5, 6, 7, 8).	16
18 prs.	3rd Canadian Bde. (9,10,11,12).	16
75 mm.	French.	1
4.5" Hows.	118th Bde. R.F.A. (458, 459).	8
4.5" Hows	43rd Bde. R.F.A. (30,40,57).	18

R.H.A. Group.	(Lt. Col. Tudor).	
13 prs.	"T" Battery.	6
13 prs.	"F" Battery.	6

Siege Group.	(Lt. Col. Napier).	
6" Hows.	1st, 59th, 81st Siege Batteries.	12.
4.5" "	31st, 35th Batteries, R.F.A.	12.

8. Under instructions from the 1st Army, the artillery of the 1st Group will co-operate in the attack and will engage the enemy's artillery.

9. By arrangement with the 1st Corps certain of their batteries will engage the enemy's guns at HAISNES and bring fire to bear on CANTELEUX and the embankment about F.12.

10. The following troops will form the Corps reserve :-
One brigade, 51st Division, in position about LOCON.
One brigade, Canadian Division, about VENDIN.

11. Reports to IVth Corps Headquarters.

Sd. A.G. Dallas. Brig. General.
General Staff, IVth Corps.

Issued at 11:45 p.m.

URGENT. **SECRET.**

47th Div.Arty.

47th Div.Engrs.

141st and 142nd Inf.Bdes.

Senders No.	Date.	
G.R.790.	9th June.	AAA

The Division has been ordered to assist the Operations of the 4th Corps North of the CANAL by making the enemy believe that an attack is contemplated from our Section of the line.   It is not intended that an infantry attack of any importance should be made by this Division, but it is suggested that we should dig dummy forming up places, and that some of the enemy's wire should be cut by gun fire. Also that any minor enterprise that Infantry Brigadiers may consider feasible should be carried out.   It is understood that the 4th Corps Operations will consist of a two day's artillery bombardment followed by an infantry assault.

Our wire cutting will be carried out during the 2 days bombardment, and the dummy forming up places dug either the night before the bombardment commences or during the middle night of the bombardment.   Any minor enterprise being carried out during the night preceding the morning fixed for the assault.   This will probably be on 12th June, but instructions as to the exact date will be issued later.

The Major General wishes to receive by 9 a.m. tomorrow the 10th instant suggestions as to :-

    (a). Best places for cutting the wire.

    (b). Where the dummy forming up places in each section should be dug.

    (c). What minor enterprises Infantry Brigadiers consider it would be feasible to carry out.

AAA   Acknowledge by wire AAA   Addressed 47th Div.Arty, 141st and 142nd Infantry Brigades   Repeated 47th Div.Engrs for information.

From - 47th Division.

Time - 6-30 p.m.

Lt.Colonel,
General Staff,
47th (Lon) Division.

SECRET

HQ 47th Div   Reference Map
              HAISNES 2nd Edition 1/10,000

1. I have consulted the O.C French artillery & we are of opinion that the best place to cut wire is between G 34 a 6.8 & G 22 d 9.1

2. It is not only easy to cut wire between these points, but from the tactical point of view, the Germans are likely to believe that this would be the point of attack.

3. The German heavy artillery will probably make reprisals — this being the case, aeroplanes should be kept ready in order that its positions may should be located.

If the Royal Flying Corps have their hands full, the French authorities would most likely be willing to assist with their aeroplanes.

9 June 15
BMC/355

Cuthday
B-Gen
CRA 47th Div

"A" Form.
MESSAGES AND SIGNALS.
Army Form C. 2121.

TO: 47 Div

Sender's Number: BM 705
Day of Month: 9th
In reply to Number: GR 790
AAA

(a) Best places for cutting wire AAA
(1) Between G.28.c.7.0 and G.28.d.2.8
(2) Between G.28.b.4.1 and G.28.b.3.5
AAA (b) Dummy forming-up places to be dug astride BEUVRY-LENS road between trenches 85 and 82 and astride trench 81 AAA (c) Minor enterprises AAA (1) Display of ladders and bayonets at the proper time opposite the places where the wire will be cut AAA (2) A feint bombing attack along the sap leading along MAZINGARBE-LOOS road (G.34.a) AAA (3) Heavy rifle and machine gun fire on the flanks of the wire cutting AAA (4) Energetic trench mortar operations against G.34.a.6.8 and G.28.b.2.9.

From: 141st Inf Bde
Place:
Time: 10.25 pm

Brig Gen

SECRET

Suggestions for cooperation in attack from section W.

Ref. HAISNES (2nd Edition Map)

1. Bombers to take sniper post in front of CRASSIER in W2 at M 4 B 9.4 during hours of darkness & turning to our own before dawn.

2. Build Dummy Trenches about E. of Dynamitiere and N. corner of MAROC. G 32 A and G 33 B.

3. Enemy's wire to be cut about G 4 D 1.3 to G 4 C 9.9 so as to give the idea that an attack on the enemy's wire in that area from our sector W.3.
(I think it is hardly necessary for us to cut our wire)

4. Machine guns to be employed from the mound in front of Dynamitiere (there is a good dug out there).

5. Support by M guns & rifle fire from the CRASSIER G 26 B. (sector X).

6. As Heavy a demonstration as possible to be brought from our front trenches by rifle fire against the opposite german front line — also long range fire with combined sights on

cross roads and comm" trenches behind forward line.

Cornwall Oughterly
Brig. Genl.
commdg 142° Inf. Bde.

4 pm.
9/6/15
415

"A" Form.
Army Form C. 2121.
MESSAGES AND SIGNALS.   No. of Message_____

Prefix ___ Code ___ m.	Words	Charge	This message is on a/c of :	Recd. at ___ m.
Office of Origin and Service Instructions.				
	Sent			Date ___
	At ___ m.		Service.	From ___
	To			
	By		(Signature of "Franking Officer.")	By ___

TO {

| Sender's Number | Day of Month | In reply to Number | AAA |

W.H. [illegible] to the supply of ammunition
for projection [illegible] [illegible]
[illegible] is not. We do not propose to
[illegible] any of the guns belonging to this
Division at the Wire cutting will be
done by French guns. aaa The amount
of ammunition required therefore depends
on the number of heavy guns you
propose to place at our disposal until
we know this we cannot estimate
the amount of ammunition at our share
required aaa It is pointed out that unless
we are given some heavy guns in addition
to the French 75mm [illegible] the effect
as regards clearing the enemy [illegible] point
of attack [illegible] be nil

From
Place
Time

The above may be forwarded as now corrected.   (Z)

Censor.   Signature of Addressor or person authorised to telegraph in his name.

* This line should be erased if not required.

"A" Form. Army Form C. 2121.
MESSAGES AND SIGNALS.

Prefix	Code	Words	Charge	This message is on a/c of	Recd. at
Office of Origin and Service Instructions.		Sent At To By		Service. (Signature of "Franking Officer.")	Date From By

Secret / WR

TO — 47ᵗʰ Div

Sender's Number.	Day of Month	In reply to Number	AAA
*356(G)11	10	GR 802	

The only heavy battery available is the 113ᵗʰ R.G.A. (2 guns only in action) AAA This battery is employed as a Counter battery but arrangements are being made by BGRA 1ˢᵗ Corps for it to assist in your programme AAA The French "75s" are very effective in bombarding trenches

From 1ˢᵗ Corps
Place
Time

R Whigham BGnl

"A" Form. Army Form C. 2121.
MESSAGES AND SIGNALS. No. of Message_____

Prefix____ Code____m.	Words	Charge	This message is on a/c of :	Recd. at____m.
Office of Origin and Service Instructions.				
	Sent			Date____
	At____m.		____Service.	From____
	To____			
	By____		(Signature of "Franking Officer.")	By____

TO { 1st Corps

| Sender's Number | Day of Month | In reply to Number | AAA |
| G.R 506 | tenth | | |

The two French Heavy Batteries in L 24 b & L 18 c are about to be removed aaa French Artillery Commander cooperating with this Division is of opinion that it is essential these batteries should remain in position until after following operations aa They are registered on the German batteries in area N.E. of LOOS & without their assistance we shall be subjected to a heavy bombardment

From			
Place			
Time			

The above may be forwarded as now corrected. (Z)
_____ Censor. Signature of Addressor or person authorised to telegraph in his name.
* This line should be erased if not required.

"A" Form. Army Form C. 2121.
MESSAGES AND SIGNALS.   No. of Message_____

Prefix...... Code ....m.	Words	Charge	This message is on a/c of :	Rec'd. at..........m.
Office of Origin and Service Instructions.	Sent			Date.......
	At.........m.		.................Service.	From.......
	To..........			By.........
	By..........		(Signature of "Franking Officer.")	

TO { _____ Continue _____

* Sender's Number | Day of Month | In reply to Number | **A A A**
  GR 006

to fail to deceive the Germans. Can
you obtain permission from French authorities
for these batteries to remain. AAA The French
Artillery Commander also asks for French
aeroplane assistance when bombardment
starts. Can this be arranged please

From   47th Division
Place
Time   5.15 pm

"A" Form.		Army Form C. 2121.
MESSAGES AND SIGNALS.		No. of Message _____

Prefix _____ Code _____ m.	Words	Charge	This message is on a/c of:	Recd. at _____ m.
Office of Origin and Service Instructions.				Date _____
Signal S.D.R.	Sent At _____ m. To _____ By _____		Service. (Signature of "Franking Officer.")	From _____ By _____

TO 47th Div

Sender's Number.	Day of Month	In reply to Number	AAA
G 741	10th	G.R. 806	

You are to continue making preparations for minor operations as detailed in ~~intercom~~ Corps No 356(G)10 aaa 111th & 112th are to replace French batteries ~~in~~ now located in L.24.b. & L.18.c ~~who~~ and will fire on same targets aaa in addition 113th Battery will be at your disposal as Counter battery aaa a British aeroplane has been detailed to work with these Heavy Batteries aaa the question of additional artillery support is being considered & the result will be notified you later

From _____
Place _____
Time 8.30 p.m.

Signature: S.E. Holland
for B.G.G.S. Corps

SECRET.

**1st ARMY CORPS
GENERAL STAFF
(OPERATIONS SECTION)
No. 356 G 10
Date**

Advanced 1st Army.

I submit the following proposals for minor operations to be carried out by 1st Corps in connection with 4th Corps attacks on RUE D'OUVERT and CHAPELLE ST. ROCH :-

1. The artillery of 1st Division will assist the 4th Corps attacks in accordance with programme already arranged.

2. The 47th Division will carry out the following programme:-

    (i) Dig additional trenches and saps, and dummy forming up places on the front from BETHUNE - LENS road to VERMELLES - LOOS road, principally opposite the salients in German line. This work is already in hand.

    (ii) <u>15th June</u>: Bombardment and wire cutting on front indicated in (i). Wire cutting principally opposite the salients. Intensity of bombardment will depend on amount of ammunition available for French guns.

    (iii) <u>Night 15th/15th June</u>: Small infantry attack with object of destroying "Snipers house" Point 94 in M.3.d. A feint by grenadiers will also be made from British sap running towards enemy's line along the LENS road in map square G.34.a, and trench mortar operations against enemy's position at "The Pimple" (Point 85).

    (iv) <u>15th June</u>: Continue bombardment and wire cutting throughout the day. At 4 p.m. some display of bayonets and ladders in our trenches opposite points where wire has been cut; bursts of rifle and machine gun fire to right and left of these points, and increased intensity of bombardment at intervals till 6:50 p.m.

N.B. The foregoing programme has been planned to coincide with infantry attack by 4th Corps at 6 p.m. 15th.

(Sd) C. C. Monro   Lieut. General,
10th June, 1915.   Commanding 1st Corps.

47th Div

For your information and guidance in continuation of instructions given verbally at conference this morning.

R Whigham BGGS
1st Corps

10 June 1915

SECRET.

To ⬚⬚⬚⬚⬚⬚⬚⬚⬚⬚

Senders No. Date.
G.R.810.   10th June.

In continuation of my G.R. 790, In order to co-operate with the 4th Corps, the following programme will be carried out by the Division :-

1. **Night of 10th/11th June.** Dummy trenches will be dug by the 141st Inf. Bde. astride the BETHUNE - LENS road and astride communication trench No.85. Similar trenches will be dug by the 142nd Inf.Bde. near the MAZINGARBE - LOOS road. Working parties for these latter will be furnished by the 140th Inf.Bde.

2. **12th June.** Bombardment by French guns assisted by 111th, 112th, and 2 guns of 115th, Batteries R.G.A. The Br.General R.A. 47th Division will communicate with Br.General R.A. 1st Corps regarding the latter support, and with the Commander of the French Artillery 58th French Division as regards French co-operation.
   Special efforts should be made to cut the wire in front of the German salient where it crosses the BETHUNE - LENS road in G.34.a. opposite Sap 16; also between Saps 12 and 13 in G.28.b.

3. **Night of 12th/13th June.**
   (a). 142nd Inf.Bde. will make a bomb attack on the Snipers House in front of the Crassiere in W.2.
   (b). The 141st Inf.Bde. will make a trench mortar attack against the enemy's salient opposite Sap 12 and a bomb attack along Sap 18 (the PIMPLE).
   (c). The 141st Inf.Bde. will arrange to simulate the cutting of the wire in front of our own trenches opposite points where the German wire has been cut. If there are any knife rests in front of our trenches at these points, they should be removed.

4. **13th June.**
   (a). The bombardment and wire cutting will be continued throughout the day and the bombardment will increase in intensity at intervals from 4 p.m. till 6-30 p.m.
   (b). At 4 p.m. 141st Inf.Bde. will make a discreet display of bayonets and scaling ladders in our trenches opposite points where wire has been cut. Bursts of rifle and machine gun fire at frequent intervals to the right and left of these points will also be ordered.
   (c). Between 4 and 6-30 p.m. the 142nd Inf.Bde. will also order bursts of rifle and machine gun fire at frequent intervals on any suitable points in the Section occupied by that Bde, especially against the Western end of the double crassiere. W2

5. The infantry attack of the 4th Corps will take place at 6 p.m. on June 13th.

6. **Reports.** The usual reports will be rendered, and hourly reports from 4 p.m. to 7 p.m. on June 13th.

Acknowledge by wire.

Addressed 47th Div.Arty., 47th Div.Engrs., 140th, 141st, and 142nd Inf.Bdes., and 1st Corps for information.

From 47th Division.

Time - 10-30 p.m.

W. Ruthven
Lt.Colonel,
General Staff.

"A" Form.   Army Form C. 2121.
MESSAGES AND SIGNALS.

SECRET

TO: 47ᵗʰ DIV ARTY.

Sender's Number: G.W. 011   Day of Month: 10   AAA

Following from FIRST CORPS AAA 111ᵗʰ & 112ᵗʰ Batteries are to replace French Batteries now located in L.24.B and L.18.C and will fire on same targets AAA In addition 113ᵗʰ Battery will be at your disposal as counter battery AAA a British Aeroplane has been detailed to work with these Heavy Batteries AAA The question of additional artillery support is being considered and the result will be notified you later. AAA ends

From: FORTY SEVENTH DIVN
Place:
Time: 10 p.m.

SECRET.

OPERATIONS, JUNE 13th. Etc.
****

As the operations will last 3 days the artillery fire will be slow except in the case of fleeting opportunities which will be dealt with by bursts of fire.

The following is the programme from 6 a.m. June 13th, till 6 a.m. June 14th :-

PROGRAMME.

(1) 2 Batteries (75's) Northern Group wire cutting on front between :-
- (a) G.22.d.9.1. and G.28.b.

- (b) G.28.b.5.2. and G.28.d.3.7.

- (c) 1 Battery (75's) Southern Group wire cutting on front between :-

  G.28.c.7.1. and G.34.a.7.7.

(2) Remaining 3 Batteries (75's) slow bombardment of front and second line trenches. Also communication trenches and after dark cross roads, and roads leading up to the trenches. Wire cutting batteries to give occasional bursts during night to prevent repair of wire.

PROGRAMME and TIME TABLE after 6 a.m. June 14th will be forwarded tomorrow.

B.M. c/450.
June 12th,
1915.

DAVID E. SHERLOCK.
Brigade Major,
47th Div. Arty.

At what hours will the Pimple & Sniper's House be assaulted in order that art^y fire may be clear of Infantry.

Reference Sheet, HAISNES, 2nd. Ed.
1/10,000

SUGGESTED PROGRAMME.

FRENCH ARTILLERY.
****

13th. June.
(1) 2 Batteries (75's) Northern group wire cutting on front between:-
(a) G.22 d.9.1. and G.28 b.

(b) G.28 b.5.2. and G.28 d.3.7.

(c) 1 Battery (75's) Southern group wire cutting on front between:-
G.28 c.7.1. and G.34 a.7.7.

(2) Remaining 3 Batteries (75's) slow bombardment of front and second line trenches. Also communication trenches and after dark cross-roads *& roads* leading up to the trenches.

NORTHERN GROUP to bombard the salients opposite Sap 12 and Sap 18 during varying periods of 7 minutes to 20 minutes as per time table attached. After dark fire as before.

SOUTHERN GROUP bombardment of SNIPER'S HOUSE for varying periods of 5 minutes to a quarter of an hour as per time table attached.

15th. JUNE
The bombardment to continue during the day as above — to increase in intensity from 4 pm. till 6.30 pm., the fire of all batteries (if wire cutting has been completed) being brought onto front trenches and lifted 100 and 200 metres for uncertain intervals (according to time table attached) and then back onto front trench.

The fire to be again lifted 200 metres at 6 ? : at 6 ? + 4 minutes the Infantry will attack the PIMPLE and SNIPER'S HOUSE.

Secret *Artillery* *47th Division.*

PROGRAMME

~~9pm.~~ June 13th.

WIRE CUTTING BATTERIES. (a) Occasional bursts of fire (except between 10.25 pm. and 12 midnight), on portions of wire which are being cut in order to prevent repairs. BETWEEN 10.25 pm. and 12 midnight THE FIRE OF THE WIRE CUTTING BATTERIES WILL BE LIFTED NOT LESS THAN 200 METRES IN ORDER TO AVOID DANGER TO ENGLISH PATROLS ETC. WHO WILL BE OUT IN FRONT DURING THESE HOURS. *This will apply to June 13-14 & 15*

(b) When wire has been sufficiently cut, the 3 batteries told off to this task will during daylight assist in the general bombardment; especially communication trenches: cross roads: and roads leading up to GERMAN front trenches.

TIME TABLE

13th. JUNE.

8.5 pm. to 8.20 pm. fire on front GERMAN trenches at slightly quicker rate.

8.20 pm. to 8.35 pm. fire lifted 200 metres.

8.35 pm. to 8.45 pm. fire brought back on GERMAN front lines, rate of fire slightly increased.

8.45 pm. to 8.55 pm. fire raised 300 metres. (quick rate)

8.55 pm. to 9 pm. front trenches (quick rate)

After 9 pm during the night occasional bursts of fire on communication trenches; cross roads; and roads leading to the GERMAN trenches.

N.B. NO fire between 10.25 pm. and 12 midnight to be within 200 metres of the GERMAN front line trenches.

JUNE 14th.

During daylight wire cutting as long as may be necessary. When this is concluded wire cutting batteries join remainder in general bombardment (slow rate of fire)

7.50 pm. to 8 pm. fire on front GERMAN trenches.

8 pm. to 8.15 pm. fire lifted 250 metres.

8.15 pm. to 8.25 pm. fire on front line trenches, rapid rate.

8.25 pm. to 8.35 pm. fire lifted 350 metres.

8.35 pm. to 8.40 pm. fire on front line trench rapid rate of fire.

8.40 pm. slow bombardment resumed as before.

10.5 pm. to 10.10 pm. fire (medium rate) on front trenches.

10.10 pm. to 10.20 pm. fire raised 300 metres.

10.20 pm. to 10.25 pm. fire brought back on front trenches.

10.25 pm. to 10.30 pm. Fire lifted 200 metres.

After 10.30 pm. rate of fire gradually increased till 10.50 pm. when it will drop to a slower rate.

INFANTRY Brigadiers to report to the C.R.A. as soon as their respective tasks are completed, when he will issue orders for normal bombardment of cross-roads etc. to continue as before.

JUNE 15th.

Wire cutting continued, if necessary, as long as required, after which wire cutting batteries take part in general bombardment which will be at moderate rate, with occasional bursts for 2 or 3 minutes.

At 4 pm. fire will commence on front line trenches being lifted and brought back as under:-

4 pm. to 4.15 pm. Front line.

4.15 pm. to 4.25 pm. lifted 200 metres.

4.25 pm. to 4.30 pm. Front line (quick rate)

4.30 pm. to 4.45 pm. lift 300 metres (quick rate)

P.T.O.

4.45 pm. to 5.5 pm. Front line, slow rate.

5.5 pm. to 5.25 pm. Lift 200 metres.

5.25 pm. to 5.45 pm. Front line, rapid rate.

5.45 pm. to 5.50 pm. Lift 250 metres. (RAPID RATE)

5.50 pm. to 6.5 pm. Front line. RAPID RATE)

6.5 pm. Lift 100 metres. Fire to gradually slacken.
Orders will be sent when fire can cease.

N.B. Heavy Artillery is employed with aeroplane observation for counter-battery work as required.

B.M. c/474
13/6/15.

CECIL WRAY,
Brigadier-General.

C.R.a 47ᵗ D./.

Secret

RECORD OF CONFERENCE 11 a.m., 11th June.

1. The postponement of 4th Corps attack on RUE D'OUVERT from 13th to 14th June was notified. 47th Division programme for feint opposite LOOS to be retarded accordingly.

2. It was decided that 2nd Division should co-operate in the attack of 1st Division south of the LA BASSEE road by attacking the hostile trenches between the VERMELLES - AUCHY road and the VERMELLES - TRIANGLE road, a front of about 350 yards.
  The right of the 1st Division will be directed on small salient in enemy's line A.27.b.10.5. The knot of hostile trenches between that point and the left of 2nd Division attack (on the railway) would then be attacked by bombing from both flanks.

3. Artillery required for 2nd Division over and above the Divisional Artillery :-

  Four howitzer batteries (4.5" or 6") and assistance of 9.2" Howitzers against Fosse 8 and buildings in A.28.d.

  Of above one 4.5" Howitzer Battery and one 6" Howitzer Battery are already at disposal of 2nd Division.

  Nett additional requirements :- Two howitzer batteries (6" or 4.5").

4. Prior to the attack of 2nd Division, 47th Division will take over Sub-section Y.1, to release troops of 2nd Division for offensive purposes.

5. Attention was called to G.H.Q. Memo. O.A.2/128.E. regarding employment of Tunnelling Companies R.E. The importance of the infantry units in a defensive line providing their own protective listeners was emphasised.

6. Attention was again drawn to the importance of reporting the action taken to deal with hostile movements when reporting the latter.

7. Necessity of the closest attention to sanitation in the trenches was emphasised.

P.S. As regards para 1, 4th Corps operations have now been postponed to 15th inst.

R. Whigham, Brig. General.

11th June, 1915.   General Staff, 1st Corps.

Secret   47th Div

RW 13   11th June

Reference 1st Corps 356(G) dated 10th June & your GR 810 the 4th Corps Infantry attack has been postponed 24 hrs - namely to 6pm 14th June AAA Your programme must be retarded accordingly

R Whigham
A/pl/s

p/Corps
11.15 am

"A" Form. Army Form C. 2121.

MESSAGES AND SIGNALS. No. of Message_____

Prefix____Code____m.	Words	Charge	This message is on a/c of:	Recd. at____m.
Office of Origin and Service Instructions. Secret	Sent At____m. To____ By____		____Service. (Signature of "Franking Officer")	Date____ From____ By____

TO { 47th Div Arty   47th Div Engrs   140th
     141st and 142nd Inf Bdes

* Sender's Number	Day of Month	In reply to Number	AAA
G.S.932	Eleventh		

Ref. G.S.919 of 10th instant
AAA Operations are postponed 24
hours AAA All dates will
be altered accordingly AAA Addressed
47th Div Arty 47th Div
Engrs 140th 141st and @ 142nd
Inf Bdes.

From 47th Div
Place
Time 1.8 p.m.   PRIORITY

The above may be forwarded as now corrected.   (Z)

Censor.   Signature of Addressor or person authorised to telegraph in his name
* This line should be erased if not required.
C27642 P.G. Ltd. Wt. W14142/641—20,000 3/15. Forms C2121/10.

S E C R E T.   1st Corps No. 356 (G).

~~1st Division.~~
~~2nd Division.~~
47th Division.

   Attached memo. from 4th Corps H.R.S. No. 214 dated 11th June, forwarded for information.

S.C. Holland Major
for Brig. General.

11th June, 1915.   General Staff, 1st Corps.

SECRET.   4th Corps H.R.S. No. 214.

7th Division.
51st (Highland) Division.
Canadian Division.
7th Divnl. and 4th Corps Arty.

Operations have this morning again been postponed for 24 hours.

These constant postponements are liable to lead to confusion regarding dates and times. It is, therefore, to be understood that in accordance with existing orders, including the above postponement, the 48 hours preliminary bombardment will commence at 6 a.m. on the morning of June 13th and will last till 6 a.m. on June 15th.

The first day of this bombardment will be devoted mainly to wire cutting, but on the second day (14th) the Heavy Artillery Reserve and the heavy howitzers under General Birbh will also take part.

On the 15th between 6 a.m. and 6 p.m. a heavy bombardment of the enemy's trenches will take place by all the heavy guns at our disposal, increasing in intensity until 6 p.m. when the infantry attacks will be delivered, if the results of the wire cutting and the effect of the bombardment are satisfactory.

H.Q. IVth Corps.   Sd. A.G. Dallas. Brig.Genl.
   11th June, 1915.   General Staff, IVth Corps.

SECRET.

47th Div.Arty. & 3 Inf. Bds
=====================

  The attached copy of 4th Corps letter dated 11th June, No. 214, is forwarded for your information and retention.

No. G/227

12th June 1915.

          R.   Lt.Colonel,
            General Staff,
            47th Division.

"A" Form.
Army Form C. 2121.

MESSAGES AND SIGNALS.

Prefix......Code......m.	Words	Charge	This message is on a/c of :	Recd. at............m.
Office of Origin and Service Instructions.				
Secret	Sent At......m.		...............Service.	Date............ From............
	To By		(Signature of "Franking Officer.")	By............

TO { 140th Inf Brig
     141st Inf Brig

Sender's Number	Day of Month	In reply to Number	
G.N 833	11		A A A

On relieving 141st Inf Brig in Section
X 140th Inf Brigade will carry out
the operations proposed for this
Section in G.R 810 of 10th inst AAA
Addressed 140th Inf Brig repeated 141st
Inf Brig

From 47th Div
Place
Time 10 p.m.

The above may be forwarded as now corrected.   (Z)   H.R. Hunt Capt G.S
Censor.   Signature of Addressor or person authorised to telegraph in his name.

SECRET.

File.

47th Div.Arty.
47th Div.Engrs.
140th, 141st, 142nd Inf. Bde.

Senders No.   Date.
G.R. 841.   13th June.   AAA

Reference my G.R. 810 of 10th instant AAA

The Infantry attack of 4th Corps will take place at 6 p.m. on 15th instant instead of 6 p.m. on 13th as originally intended. The Programme to be carried out by 47th Division will be amended accordingly.

The operations in para 3 of above letter will therefore take place on the night of 13th/14th.

G.O's C. 140th and 142nd Inf.Bdes. will inform this office as soon as possible of the hour at which they intend to carry out these operations so that the artillery may be notified.

    Acknowledge.

Addressed 47th Div.Arty., 47th Div.Engrs., 140th, 141st and
      142nd Inf.Bdes.

From - 47th Division.
Time - 9-30 a.m.   Lt.Colonel,
                            General Staff.

"A" Form. Army Form C. 2121.

MESSAGES AND SIGNALS. No. of Message _____

Prefix _____ Code _____ m	Words	Charge	This message is on a/c of:	Recd. at _____ m
Office of Origin and Service Instructions.				Date _____
_____	Sent At _____ m		_____ Service.	From _____
_____	To _____			
_____	By _____		(Signature of "Franking Officer.")	By _____

TO {	47th Div. Arty.		
	47th Div. Engrs.		
	140th, 141st, 142nd Inf. Bde.		

| Sender's Number | Day of Month | In reply to Number | |
| * G.R.842 | 12th | | A A A |

In my G.R.841 of this morning for night of 13th/14th read night of 14th/15th AAA Acknowledge AAA Addressed 47th Div.Arty. 47th Div.Engrs. 140th, 141st and 142nd Inf. Bdes.

From 47th Div.
Place _____
Time 11-15 a.m.

The above may be forwarded as now corrected. (Z) W. Luttwen Lt. Col

Censor. Signature of Addressor or person authorised to telegraph in his name.

* This line should be erased if not required.

"A" Form. Army Form C. 2121.
MESSAGES AND SIGNALS.

Secret

TO 47th Div

Sender's Number: BM 783
Day of Month: 12
In reply to Number: GR 841
AAA

I intend to carry out the bomb attack on snipers house in front of the CRASSIER in W2 at 10.30 p.m. on the 14th inst. AAA

From 142nd Inf Bde
Time 11-53 a.m.

"C" Form (Duplicate).
MESSAGES AND SIGNALS.

Army Form C. 2123.

Handed in at 3KD   Office 5.7 pm   Received 6.18 pm

TO: 47 Div.

Sender's Number: BM123   Day of Month: 12

Minor operations to be carried out by the 140th Inf Bde will commence at 10 pm

FROM PLACE & TIME: 140 Lon Inf Bde   6 pm

"A" Form.

MESSAGES AND SIGNALS.

Army Form C. 2121.

Office of Origin and Service Instructions.

Secret

TO: 140th Inf Brig
142nd Inf Brig

Sender's Number	Day of Month	In reply to Number	
G.H 869	13		AAA

Patrols tonight should only be sent out between 10.25 p.m & 12 midnight during which hours artillery fire will be lifted to at least 200 metres in rear of German trenches Addressed 140th & 142nd Inf Brgs

From 47th Div
Time 3.45 p.m.

Signature of Addressor: H.R. Hunt Capt G.S.

"A" Form.   Army Form C. 2121.

MESSAGES AND SIGNALS.   No. of Message _____

Prefix ___ Code ___ m.	Words	Charge	This message is on a/c of :	Recd. at ___ m.
Office of Origin and Service Instructions.	Sent			Date ___
Secret	At ___ m.		___ Service.	From ___
	To			
	By		(Signature of "Franking Officer")	By ___

TO { 140th Inf Brigs
     142nd   "

| Sender's Number | Day of Month | In reply to Number | AAA |
| G.N 873 | 13 | | |

In continuation of G.N 869. From 10·25 to 12 midnight fire will be lifted by the Artillery to at least 200 metres in rear of German front line trenches on nights of 13th 14th and 15th inst AAA. Infantry Brigadiers will report to C.R.A as soon as their respective tasks are completed on the night of 14th/15th to enable him to make any alteration in targets that may be expedient AAA Addressed 140th & 142nd Inf Brigs.

From 47th Div
Place
Time 6-10 p.m

The above may be forwarded as now corrected.   (Z)   H.R. Hunt Capt G.S

Censor.   Signature of Addressor or person authorised to telegraph in his name.

* This line should be erased if not required.

"A" Form.
Army Form C. 2121.

MESSAGES AND SIGNALS.

Prefix ___ Code ___ m.	Words	Charge	This message is on a/c of :	No. of Message ___
Office of Origin and Service Instructions.				Recd. at ___ m.
Secret	Sent At ___ m. To ___ By ___		_____ Service. (Signature of "Franking Officer")	Date ___ From ___ By ___

TO 47th Div Arty

*Sender's Number	Day of Month	In reply to Number	
G.H 876	13		AAA

Alterations to B.M. c 474 contained in B.M 477 noted and communicated to 140th & 142nd Inf Bri'gs AAA. Brigadiers have been ordered to notify you of the completion of their tasks on the night of 14/15th.

From 47th Div
Place
Time 7 30 pm

The above may be forwarded as now corrected.   (Z)

Censor.   Signature of Addressor or person authorised to telegraph in his name
H.R. Hunt Capt G.S.

* This line should be erased if not required.
C27642 P.G. Ltd. Wt. W14142/641—20,000 3/15. Forms C2121/10.

"A" Form. Army Form C. 2121.
MESSAGES AND SIGNALS. No. of Message_____

Prefix____ Code____ m.	Words	Charge	This message is on a/c of :	Recd. at_____ m.
Office of Origin and Service Instructions.	Sent			Date_____
By Special	At____ m.		_____Service.	From_____
D.R.	To			
	By		(Signature of "Franking Officer")	By

TO { ~~1st Divn.~~ Aeronautics 3
     ~~Adv. 2nd Divn.~~ ~~Adv.~~
     47th Divn. ~~Adv. 1st Army~~

| Sender's Number | Day of Month | In reply to Number | |
| G.711 | 8th | | AAA |

4th Corps operations will be carried out according to orders issued beginning with bombardment today and culminating with infantry attack 6 pm 15th aaa artillery co-operation by 1st Divn. and subsidiary operation by 47th Divn. will be carried out to suit above dates in accordance with instructions already issued aaa Addressed 1st Divn. 2nd & 47th Divns repeated Aeronautics 3 & Adv. 1st Army

From 1st Corps
Place
Time 10.20 A.M.

The above may be forwarded as now corrected. (Z) R W Ingham BGS
                                            Censor. Signature of Addressor or person authorised to telegraph in his name

Report on T.M. Attack 15/6/15

Report of Trench Mortar Attack

1. No. W.N.7. Date 15th Time 11.40 Place: Forse 7.
To H.Q. 140th Infantry Bde. Place ———

At 10.30 the fuzes were lit under cover of the light of a star shell. Night was quite clear but dark and direction difficult to maintain, this was done by means of pegs.

My orders were to fire as many shots as possible in 15 minutes, and I expected the gunners to get off 8 each provided there were no misfires &c.

No 1 & No 2 guns appeared to me to hit the sap with their first shots. No 4, 5, & 6 appeared to land short of german salient at first but on third shots ~~shopappa~~ I think they landed successfully on the salient itself.

No 3 gun was unable to commence ~~exactl~~ at 10.30 as a listening post in front of their gun had apparently

From

2. No.   Date   Time   Place
~~gun~~ To   Place

given some notice of their presence for what probably happened was that a party of two or three crawling germans came up through the long grass and threw a hand grenade down sap 13 from the right front. My gunners replied with their rifles & sent word back to me. Five minutes later I sent telling them to carry on. A red german flare went up about this time.

The artillery afforded us valuable protection and I think that it ~~was~~ due to their efforts that we only had about 8 or 10 whizbangs along the whole position. ~~I asked them at 10.37~~ I sent a telephone message at 10.37 asking them to raise their sights a little, as pieces ~~from~~ their bursts hit the back of our main trench.

From

3/

No.	Date	Time	Place:
To			Place

No<u>s</u> 1 + 2 guns and No 3 gun were subjected to a little machine gun fire but any <u>real</u> attempt to fire either rifles or machine guns was stopped by ~~the~~ our artillery.

I enclose map, describing the position of the guns and the spaces ringed, which were searched by their fire.

My guns succeeded in firing over an average of nine rounds per gun which with two fuze failures is more than I had expected.

Gunners reported "ALL CLEAR" at telephone in communication trench 12 at 11.5 p.m.

W.W. Culverwell,
Lieut.
O.C. Trench Mortar Battery.

From

Report by
6" London.

"A" Form. Army Form C. 2121.
MESSAGES AND SIGNALS. No. of Message

TO 140th Inf. Bde

Sender's Number: B 645
Day of Month: 15
AAA

The party of bombers under an officer left our Sap head at 10.30 pm immediately after the Artillery had lifted its range. They advanced along the German Sap. and discharged the whole of their bombs which had the effect of surprising and thoroughly rousing the troops in front of us and the enemy replied with heavy rifle fire which clearly indicated the presence of a large number of men in their trench. The rifle fire was supported by the artillery and so accurate was the artillery fire on the sap that it was

GENERAL STAFF 2ND LONDON DIVISION
15 JUN 1915
TERRITORIAL

"A" Form.   Army Form C. 2121
MESSAGES AND SIGNALS.

blown	up	in	places	which
indicates	that	they	have	it
well	registered	and	on	the
way	up	the	Sap	our
bombing	party	came	across	a
dead	German	very	much	mutilated
by	our	Artillery	Fire	aaa
The	party	arrived	safely	back
in	our	own	trench	without
casualties	aaa	During	the	night
German	working	parties	were	heard
along	our	front	obviously	repairing
wire	aaa			

From: SIXTH – LON – REG

Place:

Time: 10 am

(Z) C. Hughes, Capt & Adjt

140th Inf. Bde.
———————

The last sentence of the report of the Officer Commanding 6th Battalion London Regiment on the bombing operations last night states that "German working parties were heard along our front obviously repairing wire."

The Major General Commanding wishes to know what steps, if any, were taken to interfere with this work. He also wishes you to draw the attention of the Officer Commanding 6th Battalion to a letter, my G/229, issued as recently as 13th instant, which expressly lays down that when occurrences such as this take place, the steps taken to deal with them are also to be reported.

The Major General hopes that he will not again have to call attention to this Order.

W. Ruthven

47th Div. G/229/1

15th June, 1915.

Lieut. Colonel,
General Staff,
47th Division.

2.
———

Headquarters. 47 London Division

My S.C. 388 gave the steps that were taken to deal with the German working parties.

G. Cuthbert, B. General
C.d.g 140th Inf. Brigade

BM/489
15/6/15.

"A" Form.   Army Form C. 2121.
MESSAGES AND SIGNALS.   No. of Message

Prefix	Code	m.	Words	Charge	This message is on a/c of:	Recd. at	m.
Office of Origin and Service Instructions.					Service.	Date 1915	
Secret by DR	Sent At	m.				From	
	To				(Signature of "Franking Officer")	By	

TO
1st Division
2nd Division
47th Division

| Sender's Number. | Day of Month | In reply to Number | AAA |
| GA 79 | 16th | | |

4th Corps resumes its attack today against same objectives as yesterday AAA Assault will be launched at 4.45 pm after intense bombardment beginning at 4 pm aaa Prior to this bombardment fire will be directed during the day following main lines of yesterdays programme but seventy five minutes earlier aaa Artillery 1st Division will take part in bombardment against same objectives as yesterday but all timings seventy five minutes earlier AAA ~~~~~~ acknowledge AAA addressed 1st Div repeated 2nd and 47th Divs

From   1st Corps
Place
Time   1.15 pm

"A" Form.   Army Form C. 2121.

MESSAGES AND SIGNALS.   No. of Message

Prefix Code m.	Words	Charge		This message is on a/c :	Recd. at m.
Office of Origin and Service Instructions.					Date 1.VI.15. LB
	Sent			Service:	
	At m.				From
	To				
	By			(Signature of "Franking Officer")	By TELEGRAPHS

TO { 47 Div.

Sender's Number	Day of Month	In reply to Number	AAA
BM 32	1		

Brigade Head Qr Opsand at 8
BOULEVARDE FREDRIC ST GEORGE AAA.

8.53
1.55 am

From	140	Ind	Bd	
Place				
Time	1-30 am			

The above may be forwarded as now corrected.   (Z)   R Tempest Major

                                               Censor.   Signature of Addressor or person authorised to telegraph in his name

* This line should be erased if not required.
C27642 P.G. Ltd. Wt. W14142/641—20,000 3/15. Forms C2121/10.

"C" Form (Duplicate).
MESSAGES AND SIGNALS.

Army Form C. 2123
No. of Message.

Charges to Pay. £ s. d.

Office Stamp. 7.VI.15 LB TELEGRAPHS

AB 7 Jan 41 C/A

Service Instructions.

Handed in at _____ Office _____ m. Received _____ m.

TO 47th Divn

Sender's Number	Day of Month	In reply to Number	AAA
C 655	1st		

Reference your C 3943 of yesterday 2nd Canadian Bde will begin to relieve the right Bde of the 47th Divn at 4.40 p today aaa addressed ado 4th Corps repeated 47th Divn

858
7.30 am

FROM PLACE & TIME Canadian Div 6.45 am

W 9668/1672. 50,000 Pads. 12/14 A. W & Co. Forms/C.2123.

"C" Form (Duplicate).
MESSAGES AND SIGNALS.   No. of Message   Army Form C. 2123

Service Instructions: ACO

Handed in at ACO   Office 10.30 a.m.   Received 10.35 a.m.

TO 47th Div

Sender's Number	Day of Month	In reply to Number	AAA
4623	1		

HQ 1st Corps Closes at Chateau CHOCQUES at 3 pm today and will open at same time at Chateau LA BUSSIERE at J4A8.2 addsd all divs adv 1st army adv 4th Corps Indian Corps 1st Wing RFC aeronautics 3 and No 1 Group HAR

874
11.10 am

FROM PLACE & TIME: 1st Corps 10.30 am

W 9668/1672. 50,000 Pads. 12/14 A. W. & Co. Forms/C.2123.

"A" Form.   Army Form C. 2121.

MESSAGES AND SIGNALS.

No. of Message_____

Prefix_____ Code_____ m.
Office of Origin and Service Instructions.

Words	Charge

This message is on a/c of :

Sent
At_____ m.
To_____
By_____
(Signature of "Franking Officer")

Recd. at_____ m.
Date_____
From_____
By_____

TO { 140th Inf Bde

Sender's Number: 4.H 613
Day of Month: 1st
In reply to Number:
AAA

1st Div wish signal Section of 1st Guards Brigade to be relieved as soon as possible AAA Please arrange for 140th Inf Bde Signal Section to do this AAA Staff of Bde will move into new area as already arranged AAA G.O.C. 1st Guards Brigade will remain in his present H.Q. in command of the sub section still held by him until relieved 141st Inf Brig AAA 1st Guard AAA The whole section remains under G.O.C. 1st Div till 6 p.m on 2nd AAA G.O.C. 1st Guards Brig may call in 140th Inf Brig for assistance in case of need AAA Acknowledge & report time of move of 140th Bde Signal Section

From 47th Div
Place
Time 10-30 a.m.

The above may be forwarded as now corrected.   (Z)

Censor.   Signature of Addressor or person authorised to telegraph in his name
H.R. Hurst Capt R.E.

* This line should be erased if not required.

"A" Form. Army Form C. 2121

MESSAGES AND SIGNALS.   No. of Message____

Prefix____ Code____ m.	Words	Charge	This message is on a/c of :	Recd. at____ m.
Office of Origin and Service Instructions.				Date____
	Sent			From____
Copy	At____ m.		____Service.	
	To____			
	By____		(Signature of "Franking Officer")	By____

TO { H⁷ᵗʰ (Lon) Div

| Sender's Number | Day of Month | In reply to Number | AAA |
| AQ596 | 1st June | | |

Following appointments approved AAA Lieut Col W. THWAITES Royal Artillery (now GSO 1st Grade 47th London Divn) To Command 141st Inf Bde and to be temporary Brig Genl Vice Colonel (Temp Brig Genl) G. C. NUGENT M.V.O killed AAA Lt Col Hon W. P. HORE RUTHVEN C.M.G D.S.O 1st Scots Gds to be GSO 1st Grade 47th London Divn Vice Lt Col W THWAITES R.A. AAA Two Officers are to assume their appointments forthwith and the dates of doing so to be reported this Office early as possible AAA added 47th LON DIV Rptd 1st Div

From 1st Corps
Place
Time 10.25 a.m.

The above may be forwarded as now corrected.   (Z)

Censor.   Signature of Addressor or person authorised to telegraph in his name
* This line should be erased if not required.

"C" Form (Duplicate).
MESSAGES AND SIGNALS.   Army Form C. 2123

Service Instructions: 1st Div

Handed in at .... Office 4/ m. Received 3-5 p.m.

TO: 47th Div

Sender's Number: G 190

GOC	140th	Inf	Bde	is
to	take	over	command	of
the	whole	of	section	Y.
from	6	pm	this	evening
aaa	This	will	include	Y3
and	Y4	now	held	by
two	Battns	of	the	1st
Div	aaa	GOC	1st	Guards
Bde	will	remain	at	Noyelles
-LES-VERMELLES	until	10	am
tomorrow	2nd	inst	to	assist
the	incoming	Brigadier	with	his
knowledge	of	the	line	aaa
added	1st	Bde	septd	47th
Div	and	2nd	Inf	Bde

FROM: 1st Div
PLACE & TIME: 2.30 pm

"A" Form.　　　　　　　　　　　　　　　　　　　　Army Form C. 2121.
MESSAGES AND SIGNALS.　　No. of Message_____

Prefix____ Code____ m.	Words	Charge	This message is on a/c of:	Recd. at____ m.
Office of Origin and Service Instructions.	Sent			Date____
	At____ m.		____Service.	From____
	To____			By____
	By____		(Signature of "Franking Officer")	

TO { 140th Inf Bde.

Sender's Number	Day of Month	In reply to Number	
G.B. 629	1st		AAA

Following from 1st Div begins AAA
GOC 140th Inf Bde is to take over
command of the whole of Section Y
from 6 pm this evening AAA
This will include Y.3 and Y.4
now held by two battalions of
the ~~1st Guards Brigade~~ 1st Div aaa
GOC 1st Guards Brigade will remain
at NOYELLES-LES-VERMELLES until
10 am tomorrow 2nd inst to assist the
incoming Brigadier with his knowledge
of the line AAA Addressed 1st Bde
repeated 47th Div and 2nd Inf
Bde aaa Ends.

From 47th Div
Place
Time 3-45 pm

The above may be forwarded as now corrected.　(Z)____

Censor.　Signature of Addressor or person authorised to telegraph in his name

*This line should be erased if not required.
C27642 P.G. Ltd. Wt. W14142/641—20,000 3/15. Forms C2121/10.

"A" Form. Army Form C. 2121.

MESSAGES AND SIGNALS.   No. of Message _____

Prefix	Code	m.	Words	Charge	This message is on a/c of:	Recd. at _____ m.
Office of Origin and Service Instructions.			Sent			Date _____
POSITIONS			of HQ 47 D.A. &	Service		From _____
			To _____			
			By _____	(Signature of "Franking Officer.")		By _____

TO { 47 DIV

Sender's Number	Day of Month	In reply to Number	AAA
*BM/83	1		

HQ CRA at Château des Prés F.27.a
HQ 5 Lon FAB CAMBRIN
12th Lon Bty F.30.c.2.3
13 "   "   F.30.c.2.0
14 "   "   in reserve at Drouvin
BAe at Le MARAIS
HQ 6 Lon FAB L.11.c
15 Lon Bty G.8.a.9-0
16 "   "   G.8.c.3.3
17 "   "   G.8.d.5-5
BAe L.2.c.1-9
HQ 7th Lon FAB L.11.c
18 Lon Bty in reserve at NOVELLES Château
19 "   " G.1.d.7-0
20 "   " G.1.a.7-2
BAe K.6.b.99

886
3.50 p.m.

From _____
Place _____
Time _____

The above may be forwarded as now corrected.   (Z)

Censor.   Signature of Addressor or person authorised to telegraph in his name

* This line should be erased if not required.

8250 S.B. Ltd. Wt. W4843/541—50,000. 9/14. Forms C2121/10.

"A" Form.   Army Form C. 2121.

MESSAGES AND SIGNALS.   No. of Message

Prefix	Code	m.	Words	Charge	This message is on a/c of:	Recd. at	m.
Office of Origin and Service Instructions.			Sent			Date	
			At	m.	Service.	From	
			To				
			By		(Signature of "Franking Officer.")	By	

TO

* Sender's Number	Day of Month	In reply to Number	AAA
HQ 8th Lon How F A B. L 11 b			
21st Lon Bty G 8 d 2·4			
22" " G 8 c 7·3			
B A C BEUVREY F 14 b 2·0			
47 D A C. K 9 a & b.			

From 47 DIV ARTY

Place

Time

The above may be forwarded as now corrected.   (Z)

Censor.   Signature of Addressor or person authorized to telegraph in his name

* This line should be erased if not required.

"C" Form (Duplicate).
MESSAGES AND SIGNALS.
Army Form C. 2123
No. of Message

Charges to Pay. £ s. d.

Office Stamp.

Service Instructions. 2nd Div   8.15/a   8.31/a

Handed in at 47th Div .... Office .... m. Received .... m.

TO

Sender's Number	Day of Month	In reply to Number	AAA

Advanced 2nd Division report centre
will open at chateau MAZINGARBE
at 9 am tomorrow aaa
2nd Div am Central remains
at LES report CHARMEUX aaa added
1st Corps repeated 1st Div
9 47th Div

FROM 2nd Div
PLACE & TIME E-jm

W 9668/1672. 50,000 Pads. 12/14 A. W. & Co. Forms/C.2123.

"C" Form (Duplicate).
MESSAGES AND SIGNALS. Army Form C. 2123

		Charges to Pay.	Office Stamp.
		£ s. d.	

Service Instructions.

Handed in at 2LD Office 7 p.m. Received

TO 47th Div

Sender's Number	Day of Month	In reply to Number	AAA
POM 27	1st		

Brigade headquarters opened at NOYELLES LEZ VERMELLES aaa

FROM 140 Inf Bde
PLACE & TIME 7 pm

47th (London) Division.

Tactical Progress Report
up to Noon 1st June, 1915.

Operations. 1. PONT FIXE shelled during afternoon of 31st and Bridge damaged.

Relief of Section C.1 by 7th Division carried out.

Work. 2. B.1 Section.

Parapets strengthened and trenches repaired.

Water level at Barrier 2 feet East side.
2 feet 3 inches West side.

B.2 Section.

Keep and Communication trenches repaired.

Information. 3. Nil.

47th Div. G/51/3
1st June, 1915.

H.R. Hunt Capt.
Major General,
Commanding 47th Division.

"C" Form (Duplicate). Army Form C.2123.
MESSAGES AND SIGNALS. No. of Message..........

| 19 | aco | Charges to Pay. | Office Stamp. |
| | | £ s. d. | |

Service Instructions.

Handed in at... 3 L ... Office 12.29 m. Received 1.20 A.m.

TO 47th Div

Sender's Number	Day of Month	In reply to Number	
BM 120	9		AAA

Reliefs completed Y1 and Y2
sections taken over aaa

90.1
1-14 am

FROM
PLACE & TIME   140 Inf Bde 1.20 am

W 9668/1672. 50,000 Pads. 12/14 A.W. & Co. Forms/C.2123.

"A" Form.　　Army Form C. 2121.
MESSAGES AND SIGNALS.

TO	47th Dw	19th Lon Regt
	~~17th Lon Regt~~	20th Lon Regt
	~~18th Lon Regt~~	

Sender's Number: BM 529
Day of Month: 2nd
In reply to Number:
AAA

Bde H.Q. will close at BOULEVARD FREDERIC DE GEORGE at 5.30 pm today and will re-open same hour at CAMBRIN

907
3.48 pm

From 141st Inf Bde
Place
Time 3.14 pm

Capt BM

"C" Form (Duplicate). Army Form C. 2123.
MESSAGES AND SIGNALS. No. of Message................

SN C9p 59   YLB   Charges to Pay. £ s. d.   Office Stamp. YLB 2/6/16

Service Instructions.

Handed in at 323   Office 4.45 p.m.   Received 4.45 p.m.

TO 47th Divn

Sender's Number	Day of Month	In reply to Number	
BM 703	2	SN 628	AAA

Situations of units aaa 21st Lon Regt Hdqrs and two coys Verquignuel and two coys at Labourse aaa Battn Hdqrs at X25 C 9.5 aaa 22nd Lon Regt Labourse aaa Battn Hdqrs at L2 A 6.8 aaa 23rd Lon Regt Verquins aaa Battn Hdqrs E29 C 7.5 aaa 24th Lon Regt Verquin E29 A 9.5 aaa

908

FROM 142nd Inf Bde
PLACE & TIME 3.40 pm

"A" Form.
MESSAGES AND SIGNALS.
Army Form C. 2121.

TO	First Corps. Advanced Fourth Corps. Advanced Canadian Division. Advanced First Division. Advanced Seventh Division.

Sender's Number.	Day of Month	In reply to Number	
G.H.626	Second June		A A A

Headquarters 47th Div. closes at Level Crossing E.4.a.7.5 at 4 p.m. and reopens at VERQUIN E.29.b. 2.6 at same hour AAA Addressed First and Advanced Fourth Corps repeated First Seventh and Canadian Divisions

From 47th Div.
Place
Time 10.10 a.m.

(Z) JR Hunt Capt G.S.

"C" Form (Duplicate).   Army Form C. 2123.
MESSAGES AND SIGNALS.   No. of Message.

Lm FD BB A60 Jones

Service Instructions.

Handed in at 1st Divn   Office 6.24 m. Received 6.33 m.

TO 47th Divn

Sender's Number: G208   Day of Month: 2/6   In reply to Number: AAA

Command of Y. and Z Sections handed over by GOC 1st Divn to GOC 47th Divn added 47th Divn repeats 1st Corps 2nd Divn

G14
G.Hopin

FROM / PLACE & TIME: 1st Divn 6.15 pm

Divisional Mounted Troops.
    1 Squadron King.Edwards Horse.)   VAUDRICOURT.
    47th Divisional Cyclist Company.)

Divisional Engineers.
    3rd London Field Company.   } SAILLY-LABOURSE.
    4th   ,,   ,,

4th London Field Ambulance.   DOUVRIN.
5th   ,,   ,,   LE REVEILLON
6th   ,,   ,,   BETHUNE, ECOLE MATERNELLE.

47th Divisional Train.   HESDIGNEUL.

47th Divisional Ammunition Column.   Woods South of Chateau, DOUVRIN.

47th Divisional Supply Column.   ~~LOZINGHEM~~ ALLOUA

G.R.636.
3rd June 1915.

W. Ruthven
Lt.Colonel,
General Staff
47th (London) Division.

Secret

47th (London) Division.

Situation on 3rd June, 1915.

Divisional Headquarters.   VERQUIN Square E.29.b.2.6.

140th Inf.Bde. Headquarters.   NOYELLES-LEZ-VERMELLES.

  7th Lon. Regt.   Y.1   Firing Line and Supports.
  8th   do.   Y.2   do.   do.
  6th   do.   NOYELLES-LEZ-VERMELLES
  15th   do.   SAILLY-LABOURSE.

141st Inf. Bde. Headquarters.   Chemist Shop CAMBRIN.

  20th Lon. Regt.   Y.3   Firing Line and Supports.
  17th   do.   Y.4   do.   do.
  19th   do.   Half at CAMBRIN and half
                         at ANNEQUIN.
  18th   do.   ANNEQUIN.

142nd Inf. Bde. Headquarters.   LABOURSE.

  21st Lon. Regt.   H.Qrs. & 2 Coys. VERQUIGNEUL
                         2 Coys. LABOURSE.
  22nd   do.   LABOURSE.
  23rd   do.   VERQUIN.
  24th   do.   VERQUIN.

47th Div. Arty. Headquarters.   Chateau DES PRES.

  5th Lon.Bde. R.F.A.   CAMBRIN.
    12th Lon.Battry.) in action   F.30.c.2.3
    13th   do.   )   do.   F.30.c.4.0
    14th   do.   in reserve DOUVRIN.
    Bde. Ammunition Column.   LE MARAIS.

  6th Lon. Bde. R.F.A.
    15th Lon. Battry. in action   G.8.a.9.0
    16th   do.   do.   G.8.c.3.3
    17th   do.   do.   G.8.d.5.5
    Bde. Ammunition Column.   L.2.b.4.9

  7th Lon.Bde. R.F.A.   L.11.b.
    18th Lon. Battry. in reserve NOYELLES CHATEAU.
    19th   do.   in action   L.6.a.4.8.
    20th   do.   in action   G.7.d.5.5
    Bde. Ammunition Column.   K.6.b.9.9

  8th Lon. (How.) Bde. R.F.A.   L.11.b.
    21st Lon. Battry. in action   G.8.c.3.8
    22nd   do.   do.   G.8.c.5.6
    Bde. Ammunition Column.   BEUVRY - F.14.b.2.0

  No 8 Trench Mortar Battery   Attached to 141st Infantry
                              Brigade.

Divisional Mounted Troops.
    1 Squadron King.Edwards Horse.)
    47th Divisional Cyclist Company.) . . VAUDRICOURT.

Divisional Engineers.
    3rd London Field Company.
    4th   ,,   ,,   } SAILLY-LABOURSE.

4th London Field Ambulance. . . DOUVRIN.
5th   ,,   ,,   . . . LE REVEILLON
6th   ,,   ,,   . . . BETHUNE, ECOLE MATERNELLE.

47th Divisional Train. . . . HESDIGNEUL.

47th Divisional Ammunition Column. . Woods South of Chateau, DOUVRIN.

47th Divisional Supply Column. . . LOZINGHEM.

G.R.636.
3rd June 1915.

W Ruthven

Lt.Colonel,
General Staff
47th (London) Division.

War Diary

47th (London) Division.
TACTICAL PROGRESS REPORT
up to Noon, June 3rd, 1915.

Operations. 1. Nil.

Work. 2. **L.1 Section.**

Fire platforms made and improved. Dug outs made and improved. Mines cleaned and repaired.

L.2 Section.

New fire trench in front of L.2 continued to within 30 yards of Point 9. Average depth 3 feet. Bayers 12 and 13 cleaned and improved.

L.3 and L.4 Sections.

Cleaning up trenches, improving buttresses and dug-outs, cutting grass.

Information. 3. German working party heard working between Points 1 and 2, Square 11 c. and d., MAISNIL Trench Map 2nd Edition. They are probably continuing their fire trench and connecting up T heads to make a fire trench nearer us.

Sounds of digging heard in trench at North West corner of HOHENZOLLERN FORT.

Fosse No. 8 used as Observation Post and Snipers' Post.

47th Div. 0/31/3   Sgd H.R. Hunt Capt
                   for Major General,
3rd June, 1915.   Commanding 47th Division.

47th (London) Division.

Tactical Progress Report, up to Noon, June 4th, 1915.

Operations. 1. About 4 p.m. 3rd June, 1915, our artillery replied to Germans who were shelling ANNEQUIN. Germans ceased shelling.
Registration was proceeded with by Batteries.
At 4.30 p.m. a High Explosive shell burst at AUCHY LEZ LA BASSEE and apparently set on fire a large building.

Work. 2. **Y.1 Section.**

New dug-outs built. Parapet, traverses and fire steps repaired.

Y.2 Section.

New fire trench from Point b to the listening post North of the HULLUCH Road has been dug throughout to an average depth of 2½ feet.
Boyaux 53 and 14 improved.

Y.3 Section.

Parapets improved, saps wired, rifle rests made in fire and support trenches.

Y.4 Section.

Trenches cleaned and parapets improved.

Information. 3. 2 sheets of corrugated iron up-ended are visible at the South East end of the BOIS CARREE.
Observation post suspected in the thickish clump at North end of BOIS CARREE.
Patrols sent out from Y.3 found German patrols outside German lines.
Sounds of digging heard on South West and North fronts of FORT HOHENZOLLERN.

J.R. Hunt Capt
for

47th Div. G/51/5
4th June, 1915.

Major General,
Commanding 47th Division.

Prefix____Code____m.	Words	Charge	This message is on a/c of:	Recd. at____m.
Office of Origin and Service Instructions.	Sent			Date____
	At____m.		____Service.	From____
	To____			
	By____		(Signature of "Franking Officer")	By____

TO { First Corps
First Div
Adv Second Div

Sender's Number: G.H. 689
Day of Month: 5th
In reply to Number:
AAA

to. Situation normal aaa Nothing to report aaa Addressed First Corps Repeated First and Adv Second Divs.

From Place: 47th Div
Time: 5·10 am

The above may be forwarded as now corrected. (Z) H.R. Hunt Capt G.S.

| Prefix | Code | Words 32 | Received From abo By | Sent, or sent out At 12.28 To By | Office Stamp |

Charges to collect
Service Instructions. Priority
Handed in at abo Office 12:30 m. Received 12:29 m.

TO ado 47 Divn

| Sender's Number | Day of Month | In reply to Number | AAA |
| G 676 | 5 | | |

Please forward as early as possible programme of artillery relief reference 1st Corps operation order 88 addad 2nd Divn and 47th Divn

19/
12.35 p.m.
G.P. 642

FROM 1st Corps
PLACE & TIME 12.15 pm

"A" Form.
MESSAGES AND SIGNALS.   Army Form C. 2121.

TO: First Corps.

Sender's Number: GR.D96
Day of Month: Fifth
In reply to Number: G676
AAA

~~47th Div Arty~~ Following are the suggested arrangements for artillery relief of 47th Div Arty aaa On night of June 5th one section of 19th Lon Bty. relieves one section of 17th Bty. RFA. at GRENAY the other section moving in on night of June 6th aaa One section of each battery in left area will be relieved on night of Monday June 7th aaa Other sections on night of Tuesday June 8th aaa One section of each battery in right area will be relieved on night of Tuesday June 8th remaining sections on night of Wednesday June 9th aaa H.Q. 47th Div Arty will move to MAZINGARBE on afternoon of Monday June 7th aaa ends.

From: 47th Div.
Place:
Time: 2.12pm

"C" Form (Duplicate).   Army Form C. 2123.
MESSAGES AND SIGNALS.   No. of Message

Service Instructions.

Handed in at Adv 2 Div Office 2.12 p.m. Received 2.16 p.m.

TO 47th Div

Sender's Number	Day of Month	In reply to Number	AAA
G943	5th		

Following is time table for movements through NOEUX-LES-MINES which is being issued as appendix to 2nd Div Operation Order no 47 aaa leading battns 4th Bde move 8-45 pm aaa clear by 9.30 pm aaa road available for 142nd Bde 9.30 pm to 10-30 pm aaa available for Transport 5th Bde & ammn wagons Artillery 10.30 to 11-30 pm aaa available for remaining battalions 4th Bde from 11-30 pm aaa on second night leading battns 6th Bde move 8.45 pm aaa clear by 9.30 pm aaa

FROM
PLACE & TIME

"C" Form (Duplicate).   Army Form C. 2123.
MESSAGES AND SIGNALS.

TO (2) 47th Dn

road available for 141st Bde
9.30 pm to 10-30 pm
aaa available for transport 142nd
Bde ↓ ammunition wagons artillery
10.30 pm to 11-30 pm
aaa available for remaining battns
6th Bde from 11-30 pm

2-45pm

FROM Adv 2nd Div
PLACE & TIME 2.10 pm

"A" Form.
Army Form C. 2121.
MESSAGES AND SIGNALS.   No. of Message _____

Prefix ____ Code ____ m.	Words	Charge	This message is on a/c of:	Recd. at _____ m.
Office of Origin and Service Instructions.				Date _____
	Sent		_____ Service.	From _____
	At _____ m.			
	To _____			
	By _____		(Signature of "Franking Officer.")	By _____

TO { 140th Brigade
     142nd Brigade

| Sender's Number | Day of Month | In reply to Number | AAA |
| * G.W. 700 | 5 | | |

On relief by SIXTH Brigade you will send one Battalion to LES BREBIS to come under orders of G.O.C. 142nd Brigade. AAA. Addressed 140th Bde repeated 142nd Bde.

From FORTY SEVENTH DIVN
Place
Time 6 p.m.

	Code	m.	Words	Charge		This message is on a/c of :		Recd. at	m.
ce of Origin and Service Instructions.			Sent					Date	
			At	m.			Service.	From	
			To						
			By			(Signature of "Franking Officer")		By	

TO { 141st Inf Brig
142nd Inf Brig
A & Q

Sender's Number	Day of Month	In reply to Number	
* Q.W. 706.	5		AAA

Ref G.R. 676 para 5 AAA One Batn 141st Inf Brig will move into billets at LES BREBIS on the night of 6/7th inst AAA This Batn will be at the disposal of O.C. 142nd Inf Brig on arrival at LES BREBIS until 8 p.m on night of 7/8th AAA Acknowledge AAA Addressed 141st Inf Brig repeated 142nd Inf Brig & A & Q

From 47th Div
Place
Time 9.25 p.m

SECRET.
****

To _____

Senders No.   Date.
G.R.702.   5th June.

(Reference Map - Sheet 36.b. Scale 1/40,000.

In continuation of G.R.676 of 4th instant :-

1. (a). 141st Infantry Brigade will relieve the 5th
         Infantry Brigade on the night of 7th/8th instant.

   (b). 140th Infantry Brigade on relief by 6th Infantry
         Brigade on the night 7th/8th June will move into
         the billets now occupied by the 4th Guards Brigade
         at NOEUX LES MINES and will be in Divisional Reserve.

         No move will commence on nights 6th/7th and 7th/8th
   June before 8 p.m.

   (c). Officers of the 141st Infantry Brigade will
         reconnoitre the line held by 5th Infantry Brigade on
         6th instant. They will be at Headquarters 5th
         Infantry Brigade at LE SAULCHOY Farm, L.17.d. at 9 a.m.
         Officers of the 6th Infantry Brigade will arrive
         at Headquarters 140th Infantry Brigade at 9 a.m. on
         6th instant for a similar purpose.

2. (a). The group of French Artillery now supporting 2nd
         Division will remain in action and come under 47th
         Division.

   (b). The relief of 47th Division Artillery by 2nd
         Division will be arranged by G.O's C.R.A. direct.
         Artillery units of 47th Division not required in front
         line will go into reserve in area FERFAY, BELLERY,
         CAUCHY.

   (c). Heavy Artillery now attached to 2nd Division will
         remain for the present under the orders of that
         Division.

3.   The 3rd London Field Company R.E. will be attached to
   the 142nd Infantry Brigade and will move into the Section
   occupied by that Brigade on 7th instant.

      4th London Field Company R.E. will be attached to
   141st Infantry Brigade and will move into the Section
   occupied by that Brigade on 8th instant.

4.   The O.C. Divisional Mounted Troops will arrange to
   move into the billets now occupied by 2nd Division Mounted
   Troops on 7th instant in direct communication with the
   O.C. 2nd Division Mounted Troops.

5.   The A.D.M.S. will arrange the reliefs for Field Ambulances on 8th instant.

6.   G.O's C. Brigades will assume command of the Section taken over by them at 6 a.m. on the mornings on which reliefs are completed.

7.   G.O's C. 2nd and 47th Divisions will assume command of Y - Z and W - X Sections respectively from 6 p.m. 7th June.

8.   On relief, Tools, Sandbags, Coils of wire, and as many pickets as possible, will be taken to the new area. Bombs, Ammunition, and Very Lights in the trenches will be handed over to relieving units. Vermorel Sprayers will not be handed over.

9.   Control Posts now found by 2nd Division will be taken over by A.P.M. 47th Division by 3 p.m. on June 7th. 2nd Division will relieve our posts by same hour.

10.   A Billeting Schedule will be issued later.

11.   Divisional Headquarters will remain at VERQUIN.

12.   Acknowledge.

FROM - 47th Div.

Time - 7-30 p.m.

W. Ruthven
Lt.Colonel,
General Staff.

Addressed all formations 47th Division.
Copies to 1st Corps, 1st and 2nd Divns for information.

SECRET.

47TH (LONDON) DIVISION.

Billeting Schedule in reference to G.R. 702 of June 5th 1915.

Divisional Headquarters . . . . VERQUIN.
140th Infantry Brigade
   Headquarters . . . . Chateau, MAZINGARBE
   2 Battalions . . . . MAZINGARBE.
     1st Line Transport . . . . NOEUX LES MINES.
   1 Battn. and 1st Line Transport . . NOEUX LES MINES.
   1 Battn. attached to 142nd Brigade . LES BREBIS.
     1st Line Transport . . . . NOEUX LES MINES.
141st Infantry Brigade.
   Headquarters . . . . LE SAULCHEY FARM L.17.d.
   2 Battalions . . . . In Trenches.
     1st Line Transport . . . . HOUCHIN.
   1 Battalion & 2 Coys . . . . PHILOSOPHE G.20.a.
     1st Line Transport . . . . HOUCHIN *MAZINGARBE*.

(handwritten: Batt. HQ. & 2 Coys)

142nd Infantry Brigade.
   Headquarters . . . . LES BREBIS
   4 Battalions . . . . In Trenches
     1st Line Transport . . . . HOUCHIN WOOD. K.10.d.
Divisional Mounted Troops.
   C. Squadron, King Edward's Horse. . D.30.c.
   Cyclist Company
Divisional Artillery
   Headquarters . . . . MAZINGARBE.
   5th London Brigade . . . . ALLOUAGNE with part
                                              LE MAREQUET Wood
     B.A.C. less S.A.A. Section . . ditto
     S.A.A. Section . . . . DROUVIN Wood.
   6th London Brigade . . . . S.part of LAPUGNOY
                                              with part of BOIS DES DAMES
     B.A.C. less 1 Gun Section and
          S.A.A. Section . . . . ditto
     1 Gun Section and S.A.A. Section . DROUVIN Wood.
   7th.London Brigade (less 19 Battery) . BELLERY.
     B.A.C. . . . . ditto.
     19th.Battery in action . . . R.6.a.8.8.
     Wagon lines. . . . . DROUVIN Wood.
   8th.London(How) Brigade and B.A.C. . FERFAY.
   Divnl. Ammunition Column less 1/3rd 15.p.r. South Part of LAPUGNOY
      Gun portion & S.A.A.Portion. with part of BOIS DESDAMES.
   1/3rd.15.p.r.Gun portion & S.A.A.portion. DROUVIN WOOD.
Divisional Engineers. Headquarters. . MAZINGARBE.
   3rd.London Field Company R.E. . . LES BREBIS.
   4th.London Field Company R.E. . . MAZINGARBE.
Divisional Train. . . . . near HESDIGNEUL at D.3.d.
Divisional Supply Column. . . . ALLOUAGNE.
Medical.
   4th.London Field Ambulance. . . Chateau at DROUVIN.
   5th.London Field Ambulance. . . LE REVELLION.
   6th.London Field Ambulance. . . NOEUX LES MINES.
     with one Section. . . . LES BREBIS.
     and Detachment. . . . MAZINGARBE.
   Sanitary Section. . . . . NOEUX LES MINES.
   Motor Ambulance Workshop. . . LAPUGNOY.
   Convalescent Company. . . . NOEUX LES MINES.
   Mobile Veterinary Section. . . DROUVIN.

47th (LONDON) DIVISION.

TACTICAL PROGRESS REPORT

up to Noon, 5th June, 1915.

Operations. 1. LES BRIQUES - AUCHY LEZ LA BASSEE, and FOSSE No. 8, shelled in retaliation for German shelling of ANNEQUIN.

Work. 2. Y.1 Section.
Dug outs roofed. Fire steps repaired and improved.

Y.2. Section.
Work continued on new fire trench which is nearly complete.
New wire erected last night along gap across the HULLUCH Road for 125 yards.

Y.3 Section.
Saps wired. Depots and supplies of bombs and sandbags at sapheads established.
Trenches deepened.

Y.4 Section.
Cleaning up and repairing. Fire steps and wire repaired.

Information. 3. Five German Observation Balloons of same type as the French, have been up since 8 a.m. One towards VIOLAINES, two towards BENIFONTAINE and two near LENS.

Patrols report Germans digging and erecting barbed wire on North side of FORT HOHENZOLLERN similar to that on South side.

No. G/51/5

5th June 1915.

N. W. Webber Capt.
for. Major General,
Commanding 47th (Lon) Division.

"A" Form.
MESSAGES AND SIGNALS.
Army Form C. 2121.
No. of Message_____

Code ____ m.
Origin and Service Instructions.

Words	Charge

This message is on a/c of:

Sent
At ____ m.
To
By ____ (Signature of "Franking Officer.")

Service.

Recd. at ____ m.
Date ____
From ____
By ____

TO { 142 INF. BDE

Sender's Number G-W-715
Day of Month 5
In reply to Number
AAA

	Reference	No	G.R. 703	para
3	A.A.A.	Road	through	NOEUX
LES	MINES	will	be	available
for	your	transport	between	9.30
p.m.	and	10.30 p.m.	and	not
as	stated	in	above	mentioned
para.				

From FORTY SEVENTH DIVN
Place
Time 7.55 a.m.
The above may be forwarded as now corrected. (Z)
Censor. Signature of Addressee or person authorised to telegraph in his name.

"A" Form. Army Form C. 2121.

MESSAGES AND SIGNALS.

TO { 140th, 141st and 142nd Inf Bde
      Advd. 2nd Division

Sender's Number: G 11.716 Day of Month: 6th AAA

Ref. G.R. 702 para 6 AAA Command of sub-sections will pass to the G.O.C. relieving Brigade as soon as relief have been completed

From: 47th Div.
Time: 10 a.m.

"A" Form.
MESSAGES AND SIGNALS.
Army Form C. 2121.

TO: 47th Div Engineers

Sender's Number: G.H 719
Day of Month: Sixth
AAA

The following quantities of tools will be established in each of the sections W and X and handed over by Battalions on relief as trench stores 200 shovels and 150 picks AAA The tools for W section should be sent to that section tonight AAA Positions of advanced Engineer depots shown in each section should be selected as soon as possible & communicated to Brigadiers AAA Acknowledge

From: 47th Div
Time: 11-5 a.m.

H.R. Hunt Capt G.S.

"A" Form. — MESSAGES AND SIGNALS. — Army Form C. 2121.

Prefix	Code	m.	Words.	Charge.	This message is on a/c of:	Recd. at ____ m.
Office of Origin and Service Instructions.			Sent			Date ____
			At ____ m.		____ Service.	From ____
			To			By ____
			By		(Signature of "Franking Officer.")	

TO { 47 DIV

Sender's Number	Day of Month	In reply to Number	AAA
*BM 241	6		

The	second	Divis'n	propose	that
B?	General	Onslow	should	take
over	the	command	of	the
artillery	on	the	Y1–Y4	front
from	6 p.m	on	monday	June
7 a.m	AAA		therefore	propose
to	proceed	on the same date	(MAZINGARBE)	to
take	over	the	artillery	on
the	front	at	present	commanded
by	General	Onslow	AAA.	
I am	leaving	my	telephone	wires
and	shall	receive	new	wire
in	exchange			

| | | | 69 | |

From	47	DIV	ARTY	
Place				
Time	11.45 a m			

The above may be forwarded as now corrected. (Z) Ant Wray

Censor. Signature of Addressor or person authorised to telegraph in his name

* This line should be erased if not required.

War Diary.

SECRET.

TO

Senders No.   Date.
G.W.724   6th June

(Reference Map - Sheet 36.b. Scale 1/40,000.

1. Reference G.R.702 of 5th inst. para 1 (b) is cancelled and the following substituted:-

   140th Inf Bde on relief by 6th Inf Bde on night June 7/8th will move into billets as follows:-
   1 Battalion - LES BREBIS to come under command of G.O.C.
                         142nd Inf Bde on arrival in billets.
   Brigade H.Q. and
         2 Battalions - MAZINGARBE   ) In Divisional
   1 Battalion   -   NOEUX LES MINES) Reserve.

   No move will commence on nights 6/7th and 7/8th June before 8 p.m.

2. The C.R.E. is establishing Advanced R.E. Store Depots as follows :-

   For "W" Section at GRENAY, R.6.a.7.6 under O.C. 3rd Field Coy.
   ,, "X" ,,   ,, G.26.d.3.8   ,,   ,, 4th ,, ,,

   Each depot will contain the following trench stores :-

   300 picks, 300 shovels, mauls, crowbars, sandbags.

3. Acknowledge.

FROM - 47th Div.   X   [signature]
TIME - 5 p.m.
                                Captain,
                            General Staff.

Addressed all formations 47th Division.
Copies to 1st Corps, 1st and 2nd Divisions (for information)

47th (LONDON) DIVISION.

TACTICAL PROGRESS REPORT.

up to Noon, 6th June, 1915.

Operations. 1. Usual reprisals when ANNEQUIN was shelled by Germans. German light field gun shelled VERMELLES between 10 a.m. and 11 a.m. from near FOSSE No.8.

Work. 2. Y.1.Section.
New dugouts made. Trench deepened, and firing steps improved in First line. General repairs to Second line. Trench for reserves lengthened.

Y.2.Section.
New fire trench deepened and broadened. Communication trench along HULLUCH Road improved. New Battalion Headquarters Dugout continued.

Y.3.Section.
Traverses, Front line trenches, and Wire, improved.

Y.4.Section.
Trenches cleaned.

Information. 3. Reference HAISNES Trench Map.
The dotted line running S.W. to N.E. through Squares G.4.d. and G.5.a. appears to be a narrow foot path.
The Germans appear to be wiring from the Southern point of FORT HOHENZOLLERN to Point 1 in Sq.G.4.d. and from Point 2 in Sq.G.4.b. towards Point 3 in Sq.A.28.c.
Germans were seen working on 5th June on trench running from G.5.a.2 to G.4.b.3. along which are numerous loopholes.
The houses in A.29.c. appear to be occupied and are in good repair.
Immediately in front of the TOWER BRIDGE are four large heaps of hay. These are being observed again.
The 7th London Battalion report as follows :-
" The German Communication Trench in G.22.c. is wired along the
" South side. The wire extends as far as the brow of the hill
" and is then lost to view.
" In the triangle North-east of C in G.23.c. high wire can
" be seen behind the German front line.
" ~~At G.22.d.1, which appears to be a strong post, an~~
" ~~entanglement runs~~
" At G.22.d.1, there is a low wire entanglement.
" From G.28.b.1, which appears to be a strong post, an
" entanglement runs North from (1) in Sq.G.22.d, but does not
" seem to extend as far as 22.d.(1).
" In front of the main wire at G.17.b (1) is a second low
" wire entanglement at some distance from the main wire.
" In many places in Sections Y.1 and Y.2, there is a second
" line of low wire entanglement about 100 yards in front of
" the main wire close to the German fire trench."

It cannot yet be stated whether this advanced line of wire extends along the whole front or not.

A Machine Gun emplacement is suspected just South of G.5.a.(2).

G/51/5.
6th June 1915.

Captain,
for Major General,
Commanding 47th (Lon) Div.

"A" Form.
Army Form C. 2121.

MESSAGES AND SIGNALS.

Prefix ___ Code ___ m.	Words	Charge	This message is on a/c of:	Recd. at ___ m.
Office of Origin and Service Instructions.	Sent			Date ___
	At ___ m.		___ Service.	From ___
	To			
	By		(Signature of "Franking Officer")	By ___

TO { 1st Corps
Adv. 2nd Division

Sender's Number	Day of Month	In reply to Number	
G.W. 732	Seventh		AAA

At Relief of 141 Bde
1.25 am Y.3 and Y.4 completed
AAA Addressed 1st Corps
repeated Adv. 2nd Division

From 47th Div.
Place
Time 1.50 am

The above may be forwarded as now corrected. (Z)

Censor. Signature of Addressor or person authorised to telegraph in his name

* This line should be erased if not required.
C27642 P.G. Ltd. Wt. W14142/641—20,000 3/15. Forms C2121/10.

"A" Form. Army Form C. 2121.

MESSAGES AND SIGNALS.

No. of Message _____

Prefix ___ Code ___ m. Office of Origin and Service Instructions.	Words	Charge	This message is on a/c of: _____ Service.	Recd. at ___ m. Date _____ From _____ By _____
	Sent At ___ m. To ___ By ___	(Signature of "Franking Officer")		

TO { 1st Corps

Sender's Number	Day of Month	In reply to Number	AAA
*G.N.733	Seventh	W	reported

Relief in Section completed at 2 a.m.

From 47th Divn
Place
Time 2.40 a.m.

The above may be forwarded as now corrected. (Z)

Censor. Signature of Addressor or person authorised to telegraph in his name

* This line should be erased if not required.

"C" form (Duplicate).   Army Form C. 2123.
MESSAGES AND SIGNALS.   No. of Message

                                          Charges to Pay.   Office Stamp.
                                              £ s. d.

Service Instructions.

Handed in at Adv 2 Div   Office 6.30 p.m. Received 7.45 p.m.

TO   47th Div

Sender's Number | Day of Month | In reply to Number | AAA
G.907 | 7 | |

Adv 2nd Div closed at MAZINGARBE opened at CHATEAU DES PRES at 6 pm aaa addsd 1st Corps reftd 1st Div & 47th Div

                                                    X
                                                   120
                                                  7.40 pm

FROM   Adv 2nd Div
PLACE & TIME 6.30 pm

"A" Form.   Army Form C. 2121.

MESSAGES AND SIGNALS.   No. of Message_____

Prefix____Code____m.	Words	Charge	This message is on a/c of :	Recd. at____m.
Office of Origin and Service Instructions.	Sent			Date____
	At____m.		____Service.	From____
	To____			
	By____		(Signature of "Franking Officer")	By____

TO { 142nd Inf Brig

| Sender's Number | Day of Month | In reply to Number | |
| G.N 754 | 7th | | AAA |

Orders will be issued to the effect
that all ranks are forbidden to approach
Batteries in action and that Officers
and other ranks are forbidden to enter
Artillery Observation stations without
a written pass from General Staff
or when taken to the Observation
Station by the Senior Officer of the Batteries
using that Observation Station

From 47th Div
Place
Time 6.45

The above may be forwarded as now corrected.   (Z)

                           H.R. Stuart Capt G.S.
Censor.   Signature of Addressor or person authorised to telegraph in his name

* This line should be erased if not required

"A" Form.
MESSAGES AND SIGNALS.
Army Form C. 2121.

Prefix	Code	m.	Words	Charge		No. of Message
Office of Origin and Service Instructions.					This message is on a/c of:	Recd. at .... m.
			Sent			Date ....
			At .... m.		.... Service.	From ....
			To			By ....
			By		(Signature of "Franking Officer.")	

TO   47th Div Arty

Sender's Number: G.R.755   Day of Month: 3 Sept   In reply to Number: AAA

You can withdraw both Batteries of Howitzers and send them to reserve AAA They will not be required in front line X

X [Telephoned by G.O.C. per Mr Deedes]

From
Place 47th Div
Time 7.45 pm

The above may be forwarded as now corrected. (Z)

Censor. Signature of Addresser or person authorised to telegraph in his name.
* This line should be erased if not required.

"A" Form.
Army Form C. 2121.

MESSAGES AND SIGNALS.

No. of Message

Prefix	Code	m.	Words	Charge	This message is on a/c of:	Recd. at .... m.
Office of Origin and Service Instructions.			Sent			Date
			At .... m.		Service.	From
			To			By
			By		(Signature of "Franking Officer.")	

TO { 142nd Inf Brig

Sender's Number	Day of Month	In reply to Number	AAA
* G.H 757	7		

When heavy artillery bombardments take place in your neighborhood 1st Corps wish a report sent them showing approximate place AAA If you are uncertain as to where bombardment is enquiry should be made from French H.Q. nearest to you and wire information to Div HQ

From 47th Div
Place
Time 8 p.m

The above may be forwarded as now corrected. (Z) H R Hunt Capt G. S.

Censor. Signature of Addressor or person authorised to telegraph in his name.

* This line should be erased if not required.

"A" Form.
MESSAGES AND SIGNALS.
Army Form C. 2121.

Prefix	Code	m.	Words	Charge	This message is on a/c of:	Recd. at .... m.
Office of Origin and Service Instructions.			Sent		.... Service.	Date ....
			At .... m.			From ....
			To			
			By		(Signature of "Franking Officer.")	By

TO	47th	Division		
Sender's Number.	Day of Month	In reply to Number		AAA
BM 655	7th	—		

Bde HQ moving to LE
SAULCHOY Farm L.17.d.

From 141st Inf Bde
Place
Time 8.35 pm

Capt BM.

"A" Form.
Army Form C. 2121.

MESSAGES AND SIGNALS.

No. of Message _____

Prefix ___ Code ___ m.	Words	Charge		Recd. at ___ m.
Office of Origin and Service Instructions.	Sent		This message is on a/c of:	Date ___
	At ___ m.		_____ Service.	From ___
	To ___			By ___
	By ___		(Signature of "Franking Officer")	

TO { 47th Div.Arty.   47th Div.Engrs.
     140th, 141st, 142nd Inf. Bde.

| Sender's Number | Day of Month | In reply to Number | |
| G.H.760 | 7th | | AAA |

First Div. message through First Corps begins AAA Sniper in Brickstacks in A.2 reports seeing what appeared to be experiment going on with a cowl shaped anti gas helmet AAA Fumes were rising from the trench and the man wearing Cowl appeared to be bending over them AAA Units have been warned to be prepared and to keep sharp look out AAA Further particulars as to position and possibility of damaging action have been asked for AAA Ends AAA Addressed 47th Div.Arty. 47th Div.Engrs., 140th, 141st and 142nd Inf.Bdes.

Copy sent Div Fld Ambs
47" Train
47" Med.
47" Sigs
A & Q
under S. 771. Secret.

From: 47th Div.
Place:
Time: 10-30 p.m.

The above may be forwarded as now corrected. (Z)

Censor.   H.R. Hunt Capt G.S.
Signature of Addressor or person authorised to telegraph in his name

* This line should be erased if not required.

War Diary.

47th (London) Division.

Tactical Progress Report up to Noon June 7th.

Operations. 1. Nil.

Work. 2. **Y.1 Section.**
Wiring of gap across HULLUCH Road completed. Wire and communication trenches improved and deepened.

Y.2 Section.
New fire trench deepened and widened.
HULLUCH ROAD communication trench improved.
Work continued on dug-outs for new Battalion Headquarters.

Information. 3. Machine guns are suspected at G.11.a (2), G.11.c (1), G.11.d (3) and G.17 (b) 8.8.

Lamp signalling was observed from G.8.d.4.8. in the following directions :-
    A.29.b.0.7
    A.29.a.7.10
    A.29.a.3.10

The lamps used appeared to be proper Signal lamps.

Gun flashes were observed on a line from G.7.d.0.3 to A.10.b.0.0. Apparently a four-gun battery.

Large German working party heard between G.4.d. (1) and G.11.a (1). The party had dogs with it.

A patrol reconnoitred the road running through G.17.a.0.4. The road is overgrown with grass and weeds and in places hardly recognisable.

Half way between the dogsleg bend in road at G.17.a.0.5 and German line marked (1) on the map is a single thick wire about 1 foot off the ground. This is possibly the wire observed off ends point near this point on 5th instant. The wire extends for a considerable distance North and South of the road.

A small party of Germans was working in front of the trench crossing the road near (1) and was driving in pickets.

Germans in the main trench were singing and shouting loudly.

The ground in front of our line for some distance North and South of this road presents no obstacle to an advance being either cultivated or covered with long grass.

Correction.
In Progress Report dated 5th inst. Para. 3, Information.
7th Lon.Battn. Report. For "German Communication trench in G.29.c" read "German ---- in G.23.c."

47th Div. G/51/2
June 7th 1915.

Major General,
Commanding 47th Division.

"A" Form.   Army Form C. 2121.

MESSAGES AND SIGNALS.

Prefix Code m. Office of Origin and Service Instructions.	Words	Charge	This message is on a/c of:	Recd. at m.
	Sent At m. To By		Service. (Signature of "Franking Officer")	Date From By

TO { First Corps

Sender's Number	Day of Month	In reply to Number	
G.H.763	8th		AAA

Relief complete in Section and Command of Section taken over by 141st Inf. Bde at 12-50 am

From 47th Div
Place
Time 1-30 am

The above may be forwarded as now corrected.   (Z)   H.R. Hunt Capt GS

Censor.   Signature of Addressor or person authorised to telegraph in his name

* This line should be erased if not required.

"A" Form.
Army Form C. 2121.

MESSAGES AND SIGNALS.

No. of Message_____

Prefix_____ Code_____ m.
Office of Origin and Service Instructions.

Words | Charge
Sent
At_____ m.
To_____
By_____

This message is on a/c of:
_____Service.
(Signature of "Franking Officer")

Recd. at_____ m.
Date_____
From_____
By_____

TO { 47th Div Arty.
141st 142nd Inf. Bde

Sender's Number	Day of Month	In reply to Number	
G.H.764	8th		AAA

Following from 1st Corps begins aaa Officers at Fire Trench near L.8. report unusual and continued noise of wheeled transport moving across his front apparently in a southerly direction aaa Have informed 1/1 Highland Bde F.A. addressed 1st 2nd and 47th Divs aaa End aaa addressed 47th Div Arty. 141 and 142nd Inf. Bde

From 47th Div
Place
Time 1-30 am

The above may be forwarded as now corrected. (Z)
Censor.
H R Hunt Capt S
Signature of Addressor or person authorised to telegraph in his name

* This line should be erased if not required

"C" Form (Duplicate).   Army Form C. 2123.
MESSAGES AND SIGNALS.   No. of Message _____

Rm aaw 624

| Service Instructions. | Charges to Pay. £ s. d. | Office Stamp. |

Handed in at 6d Bde Office 18 a.m. Received 1 10 a.m.

TO 47th Div

| Sender's Number | Day of Month | In reply to Number | AAA |
| BM 48 | 8th | | |

Relief complete aaa Brigade officers
closes at NOYELLES-LES-VERMELLES
and reopens at MAZINGARBE

B4
2.15 am

FROM 140 Inf Bde
PLACE & TIME 1.45 am

"C" Form (Duplicate).
MESSAGES AND SIGNALS.
Army Form C. 2123.

HB P+ Cebo Jones

Handed in at Abo Office 8.10 a.m. Received 8.16 a.m.

TO 47th Div

Sender's Number: G713 Day of Month: 8 AAA

Arrangements should be made for the cooperation of two 4.7 Batteries with French XXI Corps aaa Arrangements are being made to place wireless at your disposal for this purpose aaa No restrictions as regards ammunition aaa Conference will be held today 10 am at HQ No 1 Group HAR sg 1027C to arrange details with French XXI Corps aaa CRA and OC four point sevens should attend aaa added adr 2nd Div reptd 47th Div

FROM 1st Corps
PLACE & TIME 8.0 am

139
8.18 am

"A" Form.　　　　　　　　　　　　　　　　Army Form C. 2121.

MESSAGES AND SIGNALS.　　No. of Message..........

Prefix......Code......m	Words	Charge	This message is on a/c of:	Recd. at.......... m.
Office of Origin and Service Instructions.				
Secret	Sent		............Service.	Date..........
	At........m.			From..........
	To			
	By		(Signature of "Franking Officer.")	By..........

TO { ~~1st Div~~
~~Adv: 2nd Divn~~
Adv: 47th Divn

Sender's Number.	Day of Month.	In reply to Number	AAA
* G 714	8th		

Reference my G703 secret information has been received that pressure pump for use with asphyxiating gas been sent to ILLIES aaa. The men working them have been issued with helmets aaa All units to be warned to keep sharp look-out for any gas preparations by enemy and report immediately aaa All ranks to be warned to have anti-gas measures in immediate readiness

Addressed 1st, 2nd & 47th Divns.

　　　　　　　　　　　H Lewin, Major
　　　　　　　　　　　for B.G.G.S.

From　1st Corps
Place
Time　10 AM.

The above may be forwarded as now corrected.　(Z)

Censor.　Signature of Addressor or person authorised to telegraph in his name.
* This line should be erased if not required.

URGENT.

FILE COPY

SECRET

  Senders No   Date
  G.S.771   8th June.

―――――――――――――

  Reference my G.S.760 — Secret information has been received that pressure pumps for use with asphyxiating gas have been sent to ELLIES AAA The men working them have been issued with helmets AAA All units are to be warned to keep a sharp lookout for any gas preparations by enemy and to report immediately AAA All units are to have anti-gas measures in immediate readiness AAA This can only be ensured by constant and careful inspection AAA Addressed all formations

FROM - 47th Div.
TIME - 11.30 a.m.

            Captain,
            General Staff.

      DISTRIBUTION.

    47th Div Mtd Troops
    47th Div Arty
    47th Div Engrs
    47th Sigs
    140th Inf Bde
    141st Inf Bde
    142nd Inf Bde
    47th Train
    47th Med
    A.A. & Q.M.G. 47th Div.

"C" Form (Duplicate). — Army Form C. 2123.
MESSAGES AND SIGNALS.

From KL 17 Glo
Jones

Service Instructions.

Handed in at 060 Office 10.25 Received 10.27

TO sg Div

Sender's Number: ly n 716 Day of Month: 8 AAA

Please make gas proof machine gun emplacement early

141 am
10.27
BM 768

FROM PLACE & TIME: 1st Corps 10.10 am

47th (London) Division, T.P.

TACTICAL PROGRESS REPORT
up to noon 8th June 1915.

OPERATIONS   1. Enemy shelled North of Sub.Section X.2 from 12 noon to 12.30 p.m. with shrapnel and high explosive.

WORK.   2. W.Section. Improvement of fire steps and loopholes, strengthening and deepening trenches, cutting grass, improving fire trenches.

INFORMATION.   3. Horse and motor transport was heard during the night, general direction from LOOS to G.35.d.1.2., then South through G.35.d.(24) to N.6.b.(27) – thence S.E. to LENS.

        During the night the Germans were working in N.5.b. just West of the road passing Point (94) and parallel to the road.

        A trench was being dug behind the hedge near Point (94). This hedge is believed to be wired.

        A strong line of wire extends from N.11.a.(19) to N.10.a.(94).

        A Machine gun emplacement is suspected on the North side of GRASSIER N.4 just North of N.4 c.a. (71).

        Enemy's line N.4.a (22) to G.34.c.(78) is strongly wired especially near Point G.34.c.(78).

        100 yards East of N.11.a.(19) the large communication trench from N.4.d.(84) forks and re-unites 80 yards further East.

        Communication trench running S.E. from N.4.b.(92) joins trench from N.4.d.(84) just East of end of GRASSIER.

G/21/5.
8th June 1915.

H. R. HUNT, Captain
for/ Major General,
Commanding 47th Division.

War Diary

47th (London) Division.

TACTICAL PROGRESS REPORT,
up to Noon June 9th 1915.

Operations. 1. Nil.

Work. 2. W. Section.

Improvement of Fire and Communication Trenches.

X. Section.

Parapet and Communication Trenches repaired.

Information. 3. German front line M.9.d (77) to M.4.a (22) strongly wired, especially at M.4.c (44) where several loopholes are visible.

A loopholed trench extends along the North side of the railway embankment running East North East from Puits No. 16. Wire runs along the front of this trench below the embankment from M.10.a (94).

A Communication trench runs down the embankment North of M.10.b (32), runs Northwards and appears to join trench at M.4.d (02).

A trench runs down the South side of Slag heap at a point about 100 yards South East of M.4.d (57) and joins Communication Trench near M.11.a (19); this trench is protected by wire which runs over the top of the Slag Heap.

Communication Trench M.4.b (92) to M.5.a (16) is wired. Wire begins about 200 yards North of M.4.d (57). This trench appears to fork at M.5.a (16). The Eastern branch runs North East to the LENS road at a point about 200 yards South East of G.35.c (34), crosses the road and disappears behind a brushwood screen. It probably joins the trench running to G.35.c (96).

Strong double line of wire runs from East end of slag heap M.4 about 200 yards West of M.5.c (82) in an Easterly direction, towards M.6.c (46).

Germans were heard putting up wire last night at G.34.c (78) and from G.28.c (71) - G.28.d (28).

Wire on line G.28.c (71) to G.28.d (28) is high and broad. There are several gaps about 1 yard wide near the LENS road.

The portion of old Communication Trench Sap 18 still in German hands is wired with low wire which runs along North and South sides of trench to the German main line.

47th Div. G/61/5   Major General,

9th June, 1915.   Commanding 47th Division.

"C" Form (Duplicate). Army Form C. 2123
MESSAGES AND SIGNALS. No. of Message

Sn HaXQ 51   HD
                MN

Service Instructions.   Charges to Pay.   Office Stamp.
                          £   s. d.

Handed in at 31D   Office 9 a m. Received 9 16 a m.

TO 47 Divn

Sender's Number	Day of Month	In reply to Number	AAA
MLy 92	9	GH 744	

Reserve gun teams now existent in Battlns in addition to those working the pair of guns at present on charge aaa SIXTH Battln four teams aaa SEVENTH Battln one teams aaa EIGHTH Battln three teams aaa FIFTEEN Battln four teams

FROM
PLACE & TIME 140 Inf Bde
              9

"A" Form. Army Form C. 2121.

MESSAGES AND SIGNALS. No. of Message

Prefix...... Code......m.	Words	Charge	This message is on a/c of :	Rec'd. at .... m.
Office of Origin and Service Instructions.				Date........
....	Sent At........ m.		.... Service.	From........
....	To........			By........
....	By........		(Signature of "Franking Officer.")	

TO { 140 Bde

| Sender's Number | Day of Month | In reply to Number | A A A |
| GP 501 | Tenth | | |

The only traffic allowed on the new road running from the Chateau toward to Sandchy Farm is traffic proceeding to H.Q. R.E. & to the Quarters) the French Artillery Commander stationed in that road has troops in not. Also the road now in troops to shell in the fields to the S.E.) the road. Had Please arrange to have these orders carried into effect. Advising 140 Bde. Repeated

From 141 Bde & R.E. for information.
Place 47th Divn
Time 10.40 am

The above may be forwarded as now corrected. (Z) R H.L.
Censor. Signature of Addressor or person authorised to telegraph in his name.

* This line should be erased if not required.

"A" Form. Army Form C. 2121.
MESSAGES AND SIGNALS.

TO: 142 Brigade

Sender's Number: G.R.803 Day of Month: tenth AAA

When you took over trenches did the French leave you any scaling ladders i.e. short ladders to enable assaulting troops aaa to get quickly out of their trenches aaa If not please arrange for a with R.E. to provide about thirty

From: 47 Division
Time: 11.55 am

War Diary

Reference Maps.   47th (London) Division.
HAISNES, 2nd Ed.
and LOOS, 1/10,000.   Tactical Progress Report
                         up to Noon, June 10th 1915.

Operations.   I.   Nil.

Work.   II.   W. Section.
                     Provision of fire steps, blocking loopholes,
                     improving parapets and communication trenches.
                     X. Section.
                     Improving trenches. Work of making new front
                     line by linking up sapheads continued.

Information.   III. From G.28.c 2.8 to G.22.d (1) is strongly wired.
                     A tunnel appears to run through the German parapet
                     at about G.28.b 2.8 into the sap running West South
                     West about 200 yards from this point.
                     Dogs were heard barking in the German lines.
                     At G.34.c 5.4 is a short length of trench along the
                     North side of the road which looks like a snipers'
                     post.
                     South of the road is a large square depression
                     surrounded by grass covered mounds. Germans were
                     working here on the night of 8th/9th June.
                     During the night of 9th/10th June :-
                     (a) New wire was placed across the Western end of the
                         valley of the Double Crassier and the Germans were
                         working at G.34.a 5.5 and G.28.d 2.9.
                         It is reported that Pipsqueaks are in position
                         in the Crassier.
                     (b) There is a ravine about 100 yards long parallel
                         to the road running South from MAISON LES
                         MITRAILLEURS. This ravine is about 400 yards from
                         our lines. The Germans were working in this
                         ravine during the night.
                     (c) At 7 a.m. 3 men were observed working a wheel at
                         Pit 16.

47th Div. G/51/5   Major General,
10th June, 1915.   Commanding 47th. Division.

"A" Form.
Army Form C. 2121.

MESSAGES AND SIGNALS.

TO: 47th Div Arty

Sender's Number: G.H. 817
Day of Month: 11th
AAA

Following from 1st Corps begins AAA.
A Conference will be held today
at 11 am at 1st Div
Hd Qrs at VAUDRICOURT AAA G.O.'s C.
1st 2nd and 47th Divs
will attend with their CRA's
and G.S Officer AAA End
AAA Acknowledge.

From: 47th Div
Time: 6-45 am

Signature: H. K. Hunt Capt G.S

War Diary

47th (London) Division.

TACTICAL PROGRESS REPORT
up to noon 11th June 1915.

OPERATIONS.   1. Enemy shelled X1 Subsection hitting their own wire with the first two shells.

           One German sniper shot.

WORK.   2.   W Section.   Deepening and improving communication trenches, strengthening fire trench, filling in loopholes and providing fire step.

           X Section.   Parapets repaired, new front line trenches deepened, and work continued on Sap 12.

INFORMATION.   3. French Brigade on our right reports that a man of 109th Regiment, 28th Division, 14th Corps, was shot in front of LES CORNAILLES.

           The Western edges of the double crassiere at M.4.a.4.2 are connected by a ridge of slag.

           Dogs have been seen in the German lines.

           The German part of Sap 12 is blocked about 10 yards in front of their barricade by a chevaux de frise under which a man can crawl.

German wire.   At M.10.a.5.2 there is a single line of chevaux de frise. At M.4.c.4.4 the wire is 12 feet wide. At M.4.c.3.3 there is a double line of wire, the front line of which is about 10 feet wide. At G.34.d.1.3 wire is 10 feet wide, at G.34.c.7.8 about 20 feet. Opposite Sap 12 there is trip wire 1 foot high and 4 feet wide.

           Along the front of Sections W and X the height of the German wire is about 4 feet.

                                             Major General,

11th June 1915.   Commanding 47th Division.
G/51/5.

"C" Form (Duplicate).
MESSAGES AND SIGNALS.

Army Form C. 2123.
No. of Message ....

BM Glos 40 ZLE

Charges to Pay.
£   s.   d.

Office Stamp.

Service Instructions.
ZE

Handed in at .... Office 5.7 a.m. Received 5.15 a.m.

TO 47 Div.

Sender's Number	Day of Month	In reply to Number	
BM 758	12th		AAA

Situation normal aaa Rt Company
A2 reported large german working
parties in front aaa Artillery
fire brought to bear on
these aaa Addsd 47th Div.
Repeated 6th And 142nd Bdes
                                  257
                                  5.15 am

FROM   141st Inf Bde
PLACE & TIME   5.3 am.

Wt.W.9668—1672. 50,000 Pads. 1584—1/15. S. B. Ltd.—Forms/C.2123.

"A" Form.　　　　　　　　　　　　　　　　　　　Army Form C. 2121.
MESSAGES AND SIGNALS.　　　No. of Message _____

| Prefix ___ Code ___ m. | Words | Charge | This message is on a/c of: | Recd. at ___ m. |
| Office of Origin and Service Instructions. | Sent At ___ m. To ___ By ___ | | ___ Service. (Signature of "Franking Officer") | Date ___ From ___ By ___ |

TO { 140th Brigade

Sender's Number	Day of Month	In reply to Number	
G.R. 845	twelfth		AAA

On relief to-night headquarters
141st Brigade will be at NOEUX LES
MINES headquarters of 140th Brigade
will remain in Mazingarbe Chateau
Repetition 141st Bde. X

From: 47th Division
Place:
Time: 3.5 pm

The above may be forwarded as now corrected. (Z)

Censor. Signature of Addressor or person authorised to telegraph in his name

Prefix ___ Code ___ m. Office of Origin and Service Instructions.	Words	Charge	This message is on a/c of: _____ Service. (Signature of "Franking Officer")	Recd. at ___ m. Date ___ From ___ By ___
	Sent At ___ m. To ___ By ___			

TO { 141st Bde

Sender's Number	Day of Month	In reply to Number	
G.R.859	twelfth	B.M.705	AAA

Battalions in Divisional Reserve are to be ready to move at two hours notice

From 47th Division
Place
Time 10.10 p.m.

The above may be forwarded as now corrected. (Z)

Censor. Signature of Addressor or person authorised to telegraph in his name

* This line should be erased if not required.

		Charges to Pay.	Office Stamp.
		£ s. d.	
Service Instructions.			
Handed in at	7th L	Office 7·45 p m.	Received 7·51 p m.
TO	47 L Div		
Sender's Number	Day of Month	In reply to Number	AAA
BM 783	12		

German observation balloon up in such a position that it can look straight down street to north of Fosse no 7 where reserve Coys of X1 and X2 are billetted

✗ 84 85A   29p 2·35 pm

FROM	
PLACE & TIME	14 pty Inf Bde 7·35 p m

W. W.9988—1672. 50,000 Pads. 1584—1/15. S. B. Ltd.—Forms/C.2123.

47th (London) Division.

Tactical Progress Report
up to Noon, June 12th, 1915.

Reference Maps,
HAISNES 2nd Edition
and LOOS, Scale
1/10,000.

Operations. I. French Artillery fired 24 rounds on German line opposite saps 12 and 13 to prevent enemy from interfering with our working parties. Good hits were obtained and parties were not interfered with.

Work. II. **N. Section.**
Wire mended, fire positions improved. New communication trenches were dug to join up with French lines. Dummy trenches made.

S. Section.
Infantry observing station in N.X constructed. Parapets and parados repaired. Trenches 2 and 9 deepened. Construction of new front line continued.
Supporting points commenced.

Information. III. Wire 4' x 4' runs West of trench M.9.d 7.7 to M.10.a 4.4, crosses trench at latter point and runs behind front line wire.

There is a 12' gap in the German wire wire where the road crosses their trench at M.4.a 2.0.

A trench runs from M.11.a 3.9 from the point where the communication trench from M.4.d 8.4 forks to the buildings on South East side of railway.

The trench on the East side of Siege No. 5 runs from the base of the GRASSIER M.3.b 2.5 to M.3.b 4.5. It is 3 to 4 feet deep and does not connect up with our line.

Square pit South of road at G.54.c 8.4 is connected to road by a screen of bushes.

German wire opposite Sap 12a, half way between Saps 12 and 13 is 4' to 5' high and 5' to 6' wide.

47th Div. G/51/3
12th June, 1915.

Major General,
Commanding 47th Division.

MESSAGES AND SIGNALS.

Handed in at 2LE Office 10.35 Received 11.20

TO 49th Div

Sender's Number: BM787
Day of Month: 12

Relief complete command of section X handed over to 140th Bde

FROM 147th Bde
PLACE & TIME 10.52 pm

"C" Form (Duplicate).
MESSAGES AND SIGNALS.

Army Form C. 2123.
No. of Message

To Bray

Charges to Pay. £ s. d.

Office Stamp.

Service Instructions.

Handed in at _____ 7.50a Office _____ m. Received 7.56a m.

TO 47th Div

Sender's Number	Day of Month	In reply to Number	AAA
Situation of		140	Inf
Brigade aaa	Sixth	LONDON	X1
aaa Seventh	LONDON	X2	aaa
Eighth LONDON	PHILOSOPHE aaa		Seventeenth
LONDON attached	half	PHILOSOPHE	half
MAZINGARBE aaa			

FROM 140 Inf Bde
PLACE & TIME 7.45 am

MESSAGES AND SIGNALS.

Army Form C. 2123.

No. of Message...........

sm H Sam 42

Charges to Pay: £ s. d.

Office Stamp.

Service Instructions.

Handed in at .... Office 8.2 a.m. Received 8.6 a.m.

TO 47th Div

Sender's Number	Day of Month	In reply to Number	AAA
BM 791	13th		

Dispositions aaa 19th and 20th LONDON in MAZINGARBE aaa 18th LONDON in NOEUX-LES-MINES aaa 17th LONDON at Disposal of 140th Bde in MAZINGARBE and LE PHILOSOPHE aaa Bde HQ LE SAUCHOY FM

312

8 15 am

FROM PLACE & TIME

141 Inf Bde
8 am

"C" Form (Duplicate). Army Form C. 212
MESSAGES AND SIGNALS. No. of Message

Charges to Pay.
£   s.   d.   Office Stamp.

Service Instructions.

Handed in at 24F Office 8.55a. m. Received 9.3a. m.

TO 41 Dw

Sender's Number	Day of Month	In reply to Number	AAA
BM460	13	G5864	
21st	Bn	section	W1	aaa
15th	Bn	section	W2	aaa
23rd	Bn	and	one	company
24th	Bn	section	W3	aaa
22nd	Bn	and	remainder of	
24th	Bn	in	bde	reserve
at	LES	BREBIS	aaa	

315
9.6 am

FROM 142nd Inf Bde
PLACE & TIME 7.45 am

"C" Form (Duplicate). Army Form C. 2123.
MESSAGES AND SIGNALS.   No. of Message..........

	Charges to Pay.	Office Stamp.
DNV ? ? 13 328 Mrn	£ s. d.	

Service Instructions.

Handed in at......H.C.........Office 7.20 p.m. Received 7.34 p.m.

TO 47th Divn

Sender's Number	Day of Month	In reply to Number	A A A
BM 101	13		

Bde hq established NOEUX-LES-MINES K18B43

328
7.45 pm

FROM 141st Inf Bde
PLACE & TIME 7.25 pm

War Diary

47th (London) Division.

Tactical Progress Report.
up to Noon, 13th June, 1915.

Operations. I. Enemy employed trench mortars against Sub-Sections W.1 and W.3. They were answered by rifle grenades and Artillery fire and ceased.
Enemy also used trench mortars near Sap 13.
Dummy trenches in Section W.3 were considerably shelled during 12th.

Work. II. W. Section.
Trenches continued towards French lines.
Work on Keeps and dummy trenches continued.
Existing trenches improved.

X. Section.
Parados rebuilt, Dug-outs filled in, fire steps constructed. Machine Gun Emplacements constructed at heads of Saps 13 and 14. Sapping commenced from Sap 16 to Sap 15 and from Sap 13 towards Saps 14 & 15.

Information. III. Short length of trench on North side of road at G.34.c 5.5 is connected with a German sap on South side of road.

Sandbag barricade occupied by snipers reported 100 yards South of Saphead on LENS road by Observer in Sap 16.

A line of breastworks covered with grass appears to extend South from G.35.c 7.2 to M.6.c 9.9. No wire can be observed along this line.

Wire along communication trenches from M.4.d 6.9 to G.35.c 5.1 is estimated at 8 feet wide.

Wire has been observed from South end of GRASSIER at LOOS, M.6.b 2.8 to PUITS No. 12.

Constant stream of Motor and horse traffic was heard last night between 9 p.m. and 11.30 p.m. moving Southwards from LOOS.

H.R. Hunt Capt

47th Div. G/51/5
13th June, 1915.

for Major General,
Commanding 47th Division.

Note. Sap No. 13 is the Sap along the road passing through the 5 of Square G.34

SECRET No 2   1/7th (LONDON) DIVISION.

Billets occupied by Units on evening of 12th March 1916.

Divisional Headquarters (and 2nd Echelon) . . . . . VERQUIN
    3rd Echelon . . . . NOEUX-LES-MINES
140th Infantry Brigade
    Headquarters . . . . Château, MAZINGARBE
    6th Battalion, LONDON REGIMENT . . . . X.1.
    7th   "   "   "   . . . . X.2.
    8th   "   "   "   . . . . PHILOSOPHE
    15th "   "   "   (attached 142nd Infantry Brigade) W.2.
    1st Line Transport . . . . NOEUX-LES-MINES
141st Infantry Brigade
    Headquarters . . . . NOEUX-LES-MINES
    17th Battalion, LONDON REGIMENT (less 2 Coys) MAZINGARBE
      2 Companies   attached 140th Inf Bde. PHILOSOPHE
    18th Battalion, LONDON REGIMENT . . . . NOEUX-LES-MINES
    19th "   "   "   . . . . MAZINGARBE
    20th "   "   "   . . . . MAZINGARBE
    1st Line Transport . . . . HOUCHIN
142nd Infantry Brigade
    Headquarters . . . . LES BREBIS
    21st Battalion, LONDON REGIMENT . . . . W.1.
    22nd "   "   "   . . . . LES BREBIS
    23rd "   "   "   . . . . W.3.
    24th "   "   "   . . . . LES BREBIS
    1st Line Transport . . . . HOUCHIN, A.10.d.
Divisional Mounted Troops
    "C" Squadron, K.E.H. . . . . D.20.d.
    Cyclist Company . . . . NOEUX-LES-MINES
Divisional Artillery
    Headquarters . . . . Château, MAZINGARBE
    5th London Brigade R.F.A. (less S.A.A. Section of B.A.C.) ALLOUAGNE and
                                                   LE MAREQUET Wood
        S.A.A. Section of B.A.C. . . . . DROUVIN Wood
    6th London Brigade R.F.A. (less Gun Section & S.A.A. Section) in huts N. of LAPUGNOY
                                                   and BOIS DES DAMES
        Gun Section & S.A.A. Section . . . . DROUVIN Wood
    7th London Brigade R.F.A. (less 19th Batty & S.A.A. Section of B.A.C.) PELLERY
        19th Battery Wagon Line with S.A.A. Section of B.A.C. DROUVIN Wood
    8th London (How.) Brigade, R.F.A. . . . . . . FERFAY
    Divisional Ammunition Column (less B.A.C. Batteries & S.A.A. Section) LAPUGNOY and
                                                   BOIS DES DAMES
        B.A.C. 15 Pdr Gun portion & S.A.A. Section DROUVIN Wood
Divisional Engineers
    Headquarters . . . . MAZINGARBE
    3rd London Field Company R.E. . . . . LES BREBIS
    4th   "   "   "   "   . . . . MAZINGARBE
Divisional Train
    Headquarters . . . . D.20.c.
    Headquarters Company . . . . PONT RYERES
    Nos. 2, 3, and 4 Companies . . . . West side of town
Divisional Supply Column . . . . ALLOUAGNE
Divisional Medical Units
    4th London Field Ambulance . . . . Château DROUVIN
    5th   "   "   "   . . . . LE VERGUIGNY
    6th   "   "   "   . . . . NOEUX-LES-MINES
        with one Section . . . . LES BREBIS
        and Detachment . . . . MAZINGARBE
    Sanitary Section . . . . NOEUX-LES-MINES
    Motor Ambulance Workshop . . . . DROUVIN
Mobile Veterinary Section . . . . HESDIGNEUL, L.25.c.5.5.
Sanitorium Company . . . . BETHUNE

                                    P. M. Toot
                                    Lt. Col.
                                    A.A. & Q.M.G., 47th (London) Division

"A" Form.   Army Form C. 2121.
MESSAGES AND SIGNALS.   No. of Message_____

Prefix_____ Code_____ m. | Words | Charge | This message is on a/c of: | Recd. at_____ m.
Office of Origin and Service Instructions. | Sent | | | Date_____
_____ | At_____ m. | _____Service. | From_____
_____ | To_____ | (Signature of "Franking Officer") | By_____
_____ | By_____ |

TO { 142nd Brigade

| Sender's Number | Day of Month | In reply to Number | |
| G.R. 887 | 14th | | AAA |

When the 15th Battn. is relieved from trenches on night of June 16/17th Battn. will rejoin 140th Brigade. ~~Instructions~~ ~~as~~ On same night 141st Brigade will send one Battalion to Le Brebis to come under orders of O.C. 142nd Bde. aaa When 15th Battn. rejoin 140th Bde. the Battn. of 141st Bde. now at Maizingarbe & Philosophe will cease to ~~be~~ be at disposal of O.C. 140th Bde. Acknowledge

From: 47th Divn
Place:
Time: 6.30 a.m.

The above may be forwarded as now corrected.   (Z)
                                   Censor.   Signature of Addressor or person authorised to telegraph in his name
* This line should be erased if not required.
C27642 P.G. Ltd. Wt. W14142/641—20,000 3/15. Forms C2121/10.

"A" Form. Army Form C. 2121.

MESSAGES AND SIGNALS.   No. of Message _____

Prefix ____ Code ____ m. Words | Charge
Office of Origin and Service Instructions.

This message is on a/c of:

Recd. at ____ m.
Date ____
From ____

Sent At ____ m.
To ____
By ____   (Signature of "Franking Officer")   By ____

Service ____

TO { 1st Corps

Sender's Number	Day of Month	In reply to Number	AAA
G.HQ94	14	G780	

Lt GAUTHERON does not consider that Germans were mining or are likely to mine in the area occupied by 142nd Inf Brig AAA He was an engineer at the mines near LENS before the outbreak of war and knows the nature of the country

From 47th Div
Place
Time 5.10 p.m.

The above may be forwarded as now corrected.   (Z)
Censor.   JR Hunt Capt
Signature of Addressee or person authorised to telegraph in his name

* This line should be erased if not required.

"A" Form.			Army Form C. 2121.
MESSAGES AND SIGNALS.			No. of Message_____

Prefix____Code____m.	Words	Charge		Recd. at_____m.
Office of Origin and Service Instructions.			This message is on a/c of :	Date_____
	Sent			From_____
	At_____m.		____Service.	
	To			
	By_____	(Signature of "Franking Officer")	By_____

TO

| * | Sender's Number | Day of Month | In reply to Number | AAA |

Bombing party of 15th Lon were divided into 2 groups. Left group did not go near house told off to them as it was being heavily shelled. Right group got into houses but found no Germans. They came under pipsqueak & rifle fire but had no casualties. Report that a German look out man ran back from houses & gave alarm. Germans expected attack & manned trenches.

telephone
11/50 pm

From
Place
Time

The above may be forwarded as now corrected.   (Z)

Censor. Signature of Addressor or person authorised to telegraph in his name
* This line should be erased if not required.
C27642 P.G. Ltd. Wt. W14142/641—20,000 3/15. Forms C2121/10.

"A" Form.

MESSAGES AND SIGNALS.

Army Form C. 2121.

TO: 47th Div

Sender's Number: Phone
Day of Month: Fourteenth

AAA

Message just come from O.C. 3rd Brigade RGA to say his 115th Battery is at the disposal of the 2nd Div and NOT at the disposal of the 47th Div aaa the CRA. 47th Div has heard nothing of this

352
8.45 p.m.

From: 47th Div Arty.
Place:
Time: 8.45 p.m.

War Diary.

47th (London) Division.

TACTICAL PROGRESS REPORT

up to 12 noon 14th June 1915.

INFORMATION. 1. Continuous movement of transport on LOOS-LENS road during the night.

Gun flash observed in the direction of N.6.c.4.6.

Machine gun emplacements suspected at N.4.a.2.2 and G.34.d.9.4.

Patrol attempted to locate isolated trench shown at G.34.a.5.5 but could find nothing. From other reports this would appear to be a disused trench about 1½ to 2' deep.

The enemy have cut grass for a distance of 100 to 150 yards in front of their wire opposite Section (W).

Small balloon which floated over from German trenches *last night* at a height of about 10' forwarded herewith.

inde Trench from Double CRASSIER through points N.4.b.9.2, N.5.a.1.5 to Route Number 45, has a wire entanglement 6' to 8' wide on the side nearest our lines. This wire is continued over the Double CRASSIER and on the S.W. side as far as point N.6.c.9.5, on the trench leading from N.4.a.5.d.7 to N.4.d.0.2.

N.5.a.1.5 (junction of trenches) and where trench from N.5.a.1.5 crosses Route 45, appear to be supporting points.

WORK. 2. (W) Section. Work on trenches to French line continued. General improvements to front line carried out. Work started on new Keeps.

(X) Section. Work continued on Keeps E and F. Posts T and U commenced and good progress made. Sap No 18 deepened. General improvements to fire and communication trenches carried out.

OPERATIONS. 3. Heavy trench mortar fire by enemy opposite (W) Section stopped by 19th London Battery.

Enemy shelled dummy trenches and our front line during 13th and 14th.

J R Hunt Capt
for

Major General,
Commanding 47th (London) Div.

14th June 1915.
G/61/6.

"C" Form (Duplicate).
MESSAGES AND SIGNALS.   Army Form C. 2123.

No. of Message

Charges to Pay.   Office Stamp
£   s.   d.

Y 15.VI.15. LB
TELEGRAPHS

Service Instructions.
aeo   12.25

Handed in at _____ Office _____ m. Received _____ m.

TO 47th Division

Sender's Number	Day of Month	In reply to Number	AAA
G793	15.		

Following received from AdV 1st
Army begins Air reports from
4.45 to 7 show pronounced
railway movement DOUAI to LILLE
via SECLIN aaa this is
either return of stock which
moved southwards from COURTRAI yesterday
or movement of reinforcements to
LILLE aaa former alternative is
more probable aaa there is
also considerable movement on LILLE
DON PROVIN line aaa focus
of the movement is DON
aaa it is probably reinforcements
to NEUVE CHAPELLE - LA BASSEE
section aaa extent of movements
not yet known but unlikely

FROM
PLACE & TIME

364
12.40 pm

Wt.W.9662—1672. 50,000 Pads. 1584—1/15. S. B. Ltd.—Forms/C.2123.

"C" Form (Duplicate). Army Form
MESSAGES AND SIGNALS. No. of Message

Charges to Pay. Office Stamp.
£ s. d. 15.VI.15

Service Instructions.

Handed in at .... Office .... m. Received .... m.

TO (2) 47 Div:

Sender's Number	Day of Month	In reply to Number	A A A
to proceed	1	regiment	ends

FROM 1st Corps
PLACE & TIME 12.15 pm

"C" Form (Duplicate). Army Form C.2123.
MESSAGES AND SIGNALS. No. of Message

Sn OC hm 141

Charges to Pay. Office Stamp.

Service Instructions.

Handed in at 2 LF Office 3.15 p.m. Received 3.36 p.m.

TO 47th Div

Sender's Number	Day of Month	In reply to Number	AAA
BM 119	16	GH 902	
About	10.45	pm	bombing parties
succeeded in	reaching within ten		
yards of	the	allotted	houses
when enemy	opened	heavy	shrapnel
and	HE	shell	fire	on
the	line	of	the
houses	aaa	This	was	followed
by	heavy	rifle	fire	for
twelve	minutes	all	along	the
line	aaa	Hostile	trenches	were
evidently	strongly	manned and	a
look-out post	from	the	nearest
house	to	this	line	must
have	given	the	alarm	aaa
After	the	fire	died	down
it	was	considered by	the
OC	bombing	party	that	no

FROM
PLACE & TIME

265
3.40 pm

"C" Form (Duplicate).
MESSAGES AND SIGNALS.

Army Form C.2123.

No. of Message

Charges to Pay. £ s. d.

Office Stamp.

Service Instructions: *paper*

Handed in at _____ Office _____ m. Received 3.36 p.m.

TO Bde 2

Sender's Number | Day of Month | In reply to Number | AAA

germans were in the house so the bombing party withdrew aaa 66 15th Battn reported their return at 11.45 pm forwarded to me and I the report to you and the CRA by 11.50 pm aaa there was there were no casualties in the bombing party aaa

FROM PLACE & TIME: 142nd Inf Bde 3.10 pm

"A" Form. Army Form C. 2121.

MESSAGES AND SIGNALS.

No. of Message _____

Prefix ___ Code ___ m.	Words	Charge	This message is on a/c of:	Recd. at ___ m.
Office of Origin and Service Instructions.	Sent			Date ___
	At ___ m.		___ Service.	From ___
	To ___			
	By ___		(Signature of "Franking Officer")	By ___

TO { 142nd Inf Brig

| Sender's Number | Day of Month | In reply to Number | AAA |
| Y.R.905 | 15th | | |

The Major General wishes you to consider
the possibility of connecting our line
near Sap 18 with the MAISON LES
MITRAILLEURS and thus reducing the
length of front to be held AAA Please
report as soon as possible the amount
of work which would be required to
make this new line of trench and
give your opinion as to the ~~feasibility~~
~~of~~ desirability of joining these two
points

From 47th Div
Place
Time 3.40 p.m.

The above may be forwarded as now corrected.   (Z)

Censor. Signature of Addressor or person authorised to telegraph in his name

* This line should be erased if not required.

"A" Form. Army Form C. 2121.

MESSAGES AND SIGNALS.   No. of Message _____

Prefix ___ Code ___ m.	Words	Charge	This message is on a/c of:	Rec'd. at ___ m.
Office of Origin and Service Instructions.	Sent			Date ___
	At ___ m.		___ Service.	From ___
	To ___			
	By ___		(Signature of "Franking Officer")	By ___

TO { 1st Corps
     Adv. 2nd Div.

| Sender's Number | Day of Month | In reply to Number | |
| G.H. 908 | Fifteenth | | AAA |

At 3.55 p.m. enemy shelled X1 on account of display of bayonets and ladders AAA French Artillery replied effectively AAA Bursts of rifle and machine gun fire have been opened in Section W AAA Shelling in this section has not been heavy AAA No change in Divisional or Brigade Headquarters AAA Addressed First Corps repeated Adv. 2nd Div.

From: 47th Div.
Place:
Time: 5.37 p.m.

The above may be forwarded as now corrected. (Z)

Censor. J.H.R. Hunt Capt G.S.
Signature of Addresser or person authorised to telegraph in his name

* This line should be erased if not required.

"A" Form. Army Form C. 2121.

MESSAGES AND SIGNALS.

TO C.R.A.

Sender's Number: A.R.911 Day of Month: 15th

The Major General wishes you to convey to Colonel Muller O the French Artillery cooperating with this Division his high appreciation of the work they have done during the last few days and the heavy fire brought to bear on the German trenches fully attained its object in causing the enemy to believe that an attack was to be made upon this section thus materially assisting the attack of 4th Corps and the General is most grateful to Colonel Muller for his devotion.

From: 47th Division
Time: 9 pm

Mullen Lt Col

"A" Form.
MESSAGES AND SIGNALS.
Army Form C. 2121.
No. of Message _____

Prefix ____ Code ____ m.	Words	Charge	This message is on a/c of :	Recd. at ____ m.
Office of Origin and Service Instructions.	Sent			Date ____
	At ____ m.		Service.	From ____
	To			
	By	(Signature of "Franking Officer")	By ____	

TO { 47 Div Mtd Troops
47 Div Engrs. 47th Div. Sigs
140 Inf Bde. Train. Med. A. & Q.

Sender's Number: G.H. 912
Day of Month: 15th
In reply to Number:
AAA

Observing Officers state that the Canadians have taken German Second Line of Trenches 4 to 4.15 AAA 7th Div have captured first line and are working up towards Second line AAA 51st Div have reached North corner of RUE D'OUVERT and are bombing down it AAA This has not yet been officially confirmed AAA Up to then no intense German Artillery fire had been brought to bear on our troops which First Corps attribute to the operations of this Division

From: 47th Div
Place:
Time: 6-10 pm

The above may be forwarded as now corrected. (Z)
Censor. Signature of Addresser or person authorised to telegraph in his name
* This line should be erased if not required.

"C" Form (Duplicate).
MESSAGES AND SIGNALS.
Army Form C.2123.
No. of Message

NWS 62
W.

Charges to Pay.
£ s. d.

Office Stamp.
15.VI.15. LB

Service Instructions.

Handed in at _GHQ_ Office _8.52_ m. Received _9.8_ m.

TO _Adv 47th Divn_

Sender's Number: G 797　　Day of Month: 15th　　In reply to Number:　　AAA

1st Army report aaa Recon begins following reports received up to 7.30 pm aaa Canadian Divn 2nd Canadian Bde in front German trench at 6.20 pm aaa Canadian infantry seen bombing towards H5 aaa 7th Divn right company made lodge in German first line trench 6.25 aaa first of — O — O reports left company do in German line trench same from aaa Germans seen leaving trench 8.15 to I.19 aaa 51st Divn 2 xxxxxx captured 4 infantry seen running towards 90 heavy fire 625 pm
376
9.17 pm

FROM
PLACE & TIME

"C" Form (Duplicate). Army Form C. 2123.
MESSAGES AND SIGNALS. No. of Message _____

	Charges to Pay.	Office Stamp.
	£ s. d	Y 15. VI.
Service Instructions.		TELEGRAPHS

Handed in at _____ Office _____ m. Received _____ m.

TO ②

Sender's Number	Day of Month	In reply to Number	AAA
aaa	from HQ	seen east	
of	WILLOWS east	of 6.45 pm	29
aaa	another L10		
combine	Indian Corps	attack	of
not	parts	on V.3 did	
1st	succeed aaa	feint by	
successfully	Corps about	FOSSE	no
turns	own enemys	artillery fire	
	addressed 1st	2nd	47th
		Aeronautics 3	

FROM 1st Corps
PLACE & TIME 8.45 pm

Wt. W.9668—1672. 50,000 Pads. 1584—1/15. S.B. Ltd.—Forms/C.2123.

"C" Form (Duplicate).
MESSAGES AND SIGNALS. Army Form C. 2123.

From KB 33

Handed in at 3LD Office 10·20 pm Received 10·43 pm

TO 47 Div

Sender's Number	Day of Month	In reply to Number	AAA
SC 518	15	—	

OC XI report german scaling ladders distinctly seen in artillery section 9.⅔ opposite sap 16 aaa artillery informed aaa great vigilance ordered aaa

378
10·47

FROM 140 Inf Bde
PLACE & TIME 10·20 pm

Reference Map
HAISNES 2nd Ed. and
LOOS - Scale
1/10,000.

War Diary

47th (London) Division.

Tactical Progress Report
up to Noon, June 15th, 1915.

Operations. I. The bombing parties sent out last night to SNIPERS HOUSE and SAP 18 caused the Germans to man their front trenches. SNIPERS HOUSE was found empty.

The only German corpse found in SAP 18 was mangled to such an extent that it was impossible to ascertain the regiment to which the man belonged. A noticeable point is that there was very little Machine Gun fire from the German lines. Their rifle fire was wild and high.

Work. II. W. Section.

Repairs to parapets. Communication trench in SAP 1 deepened. Work continued on trench joining up with French. Work continued on Keep A and commenced on Keep B.

X. Section.

Trenches repaired. SAP 18 cleaned and rebuilt. Fire trenches improved. Trench number 16 cleared and made capable of use as a communication trench. Work continued on Posts E, F, G and H. Transport again heard in rear of German lines.

Information. III. Trench running from SIEGE No. 5 to B of M.3.B is 3 feet deep near CRASSIER and 1 foot deep at M.3.b 5.4.

New German sap observed South of Double CRASSIER at M.4.c 4.9 running out about 5 yards. Parapet at end appears to have two loopholes.

Gap in wire at M.4.a 2.2 has been closed to about 3 feet. The path through gap appears well worn.

There appears to be an earthwork at G.35.c 4.3 in East angle of cross roads concealed from our front by a house with an iron roof.

High wire seen in front of trench running West of LOOS CEMETERY from G.35.c 9.6 to G.35.a 7.2. Description of wire not yet reported.

Wire previously reported from M.6.b 2.8 appears to run South West to M.6.c 4.6. At about M.6.b 0.3 it passes East of deep chalk pit and from here to M.6.c 4.6 in front of a line of thick bushes.

47th Div. G/51/5

15th June, 1915.

J.R. Stunt Capt
for Major General,
Commanding 47th (London) Divn.

"C" Form (Duplicate).   Army Form C. 2123.
MESSAGES AND SIGNALS.

Handed in at aco Office 7.7 p.m. Received m.

TO: 47 Div'n

Sender's Number: G 801 Day of Month: 16th AAA

Heavy bombing counter attack compelled our troops to withdraw from those positions gained last night north of Canal

FROM: 1st Corps
PLACE & TIME: 7.5 a.m.

MESSAGES AND SIGNALS.

M JKW 180 aco

Handed in at aco Office 9.53 a.m. Received 10.12 A

TO Adv 47th Divn

Sender's Number: G 802 Day of Month: 16th

AAA

1st Army report begins Early in the night that portion of the 7th divn between H3 and J4 was attacked by the Germans and driven back to our own lines aaa Subsequently the Canadians about H2 – H5 were forced to withdraw aaa at 3 am 51st Div reported that their right had been bombed out of K6 and J2 and had withdrawn to our own lines aaa Similarly left of 7th Divn at J-11-J13 were bombed out aaa This left Grenadiers at J10 with both

387

10.15 am

Form (Duplicate).
MESSAGES AND SIGNALS.

Service Instructions.

Handed in at _aco_ Office _9.5_ m. Received _____ m.

TO (2) adv 47 Div

			AAA
flanks	exposed	and	they	also
were	forced	back aaa	about
5	am	report	received	from
51st	Div	that	troops	which
had	captured	L9	and	L10
were	unable	to	retain	points
captured	and	were	withdrawing	then
to	original	line aaa	Germans
in	considerable	strength aaa	2nd
Army	report	that	enemys	trenches
running	now	from	Hooge	Chateau
to	YPRES	– Roulers	railway	had
been	penetrated	at	various	points
aaa	further	telegram	from	1st
Army	states	that	Second	Army
have	made	further	progress	and
have	taken	111	prisoners aaa

FROM
PLACE & TIME 1st Corps 9.35 am

"A" Form.   Army Form C. 2121.
MESSAGES AND SIGNALS.

TO	140th	Inf.	Bde
	141st	Inf.	Bde.
	142nd	Inf.	Bde.

Sender's Number	Day of Month	In reply to Number	AAA
*G.H.924	16th		

Under instructions from 1st Corps NO reliefs will take place tonight. aaa Acknowledge. AAA. addressed 140th 141st and 142nd Inf. Bde.

From 47th Div
Time 5.25 pm

H.R. Hunt Capt G.S.

"C" Form (Duplicate).
MESSAGES AND SIGNALS.

Army Form C. 2123.

ACO

Service Instructions.
Handed in at .... Office ...... m. Received ...... m.

TO 47th Div

Sender's Number Day of Month In reply to Number AAA
9404   16

1st Army report at 5.45
pm that French attack has
captured front line of German
trenches along nearly all the
front & has progressed further
in many places aaa observers
report having seen French infantry
on crest of ridge SE
of SOUCHEZ

FROM 1st Corps
PLACE & TIME 6.5 pm

"C" Form (Duplicate).
MESSAGES AND SIGNALS.

Army Form C.
No. of Message

Charges to Pay.
£   s.

Office Stamp.
Y 18. VI. 15. L3
TELEGRAPHS

Service Instructions.

Handed in at _____ Office ____ m. Received ____ m.

TO 47th Divn

Sender's Number	Day of Month	In reply to Number	AAA
Reports	received	5.45 pm	shows
that	8	Liverpools have occupied	
German	trenches	at	L10 &
Scots	Fusiliers at	I2–I4	
GH 930		4.00	
		7-4 pm	

FROM
PLACE & TIME   1st Corps
7.0 pm

"A" Form. Army Form C. 2121.

MESSAGES AND SIGNALS. No. of Message _____

Prefix ___ Code ___ m.	Words	Charge	This message is on a/c of:	Recd. at ___ m.
Office of Origin and Service Instructions.	Sent			Date ___
	At ___ m.		Service	From ___
	To ___			
	By ___		(Signature of "Franking Officer.")	By ___

URGENT **SECRET**

TO { 47th Div Mounted Troops   47th Div Arty
     47th Div Engrs 140th Inf Bde   141st Inf Bde
     142nd Inf Bde

| Sender's Number | Day of Month | In reply to Number | **AAA** |
| G.R.929 | Sixteenth | | |

1st Corps warns 47th Div that it should be on its guard against a German counter-attack from the direction of LOOS tonight AAA All units in Divisional Reserve will be ready to move off at half an hours notice AAA Battalion of 141st Inf Bde at NOEUX LES MINES will move to MAZINGARBE at once AAA Addressed 47th Div Mounted Troops, Arty, Engrs and 140th 141st and 142nd Inf Bdes AAA   Acknowledge

From	47th Div.		
Place			
Time	7.45 p.m.		

The above may be forwarded as now corrected. (Z)
.... (Sgd) H.R. HUNT Capt. G.S.
    Censor.   Signature of Addressor or person authorised to telegraph in his name.

* This line should be erased if not required.

"C" Form (Duplicate).   Army Form C. 2123.
MESSAGES AND SIGNALS.

Service Instructions.

Handed in at _GHQ_ Office ___ m. Received _7.47_ m.

TO _17th Div._

Sender's Number	Day of Month	In reply to Number	AAA
G4B	16		

2nd Army reports situation about 7pm as follows aaa on right advance of 149th Bde was checked & owing to wire no progress from HOOGE had as yet been possible aaa in centre 3rd Div had occupied enemy first line aaa own line driven back temporarily by shell fire from BELLEWARDE FARM but on left own troops holding 250 yards German second line trenches aaa one Bde moving up to attack line BELLEWARDE LAKE to BELLEWARDE FARM aaa German counter attack launched from N of

FROM _H 01_

PLACE & TIME _7.47 pm_

Wt.W.9668—1672. 50,000 Pads. 1584—1/15. S. B. Ltd.—Forms/C.2123.

"C" Form (Duplicate).
Army Form C. 2123.

MESSAGES AND SIGNALS.

No. of Message

Office Stamp.

Service Instructions.

Handed in at _____ Office _____ m. Received _____ m.

TO   Z. 47th Div

| Sender's Number | Day of Month | In reply to Number | AAA |

BELLEWARDE LAKE Ridge down many
dead being left on ground
aaa up to 12 noon
159 prisoners has reached 3rd
Div HQ

7.47 pm

FROM   1st Corps
PLACE & TIME   7.20 pm

"A" Form.
MESSAGES AND SIGNALS.
Army Form C. 2121.

Prefix	Code	Words	Charge	This message is on a/c of:	Recd. at ... m.
Office of Origin and Service Instructions.		Sent At ... m. To By	**SECRET**	Service. (Signature of "Franking Officer.")	Date From By

TO { 47th Div.Arty.   47th Div.Engrs.   47th Div.Mtd.Tps.
140th, 141st, 142nd Inf. Bde.

Sender's Number	Day of Month	In reply to Number	**AAA**
G.R. 934	16th		

In continuation of G.R. 929. AAA Under instructions from 1st Corps every precaution must be taken to deal promptly with hostile counter-attacks especially from direction of LOOS AAA 1st Guards Bde. and 6th Inf. Bde. are in Corps Reserve and are to be in readiness to move at one hours notice till further orders AAA Battalions of 6th Inf.Bde. in vicinity of VAUDRICOURT and VERQUIN are to be prepared to move to MAZINGARBE AAA The closest touch must be maintained with the French on our right and arrangements must be made to support their left AAA 141st Inf.Bde. will get into touch with 92nd French Division at LES BREBIS with a view to giving immediate support to the French left if such support is asked for AAA Acknowledge.

From 47th Div.
Place
Time 10 P.M.

"C" Form (Duplicate).
MESSAGES AND SIGNALS.

Army Form C.2123
No. of Message

Charges to Pay. 2 s. d.

Office Stamp.

JM GK+ 18   NP
            Bray

Service Instructions.

Handed in at 720   Office 9.52 P.m.   Received 10.22 P.m.

TO   47 Div

Sender's Number	Day of Month	In reply to Number	AAA
Bm 860	16th	GQ 929	

Received aaa Bde HQ established Chateau MAZINGARBE

407
10.30 pm

FROM PLACE & TIME   141 Inf Bde
9-47 pm

"C" Form (Duplicate). Army Form C. 2123.
MESSAGES AND SIGNALS.   No. of Message

To HK 98   aco   Charges to Pay.   Office Stamp.
           Cunningham

Service Instructions.

Handed in at aco   Office 10.30 p.m.   Received 10.39 p.m.

TO   47 Divn

Sender's Number | Day of Month | In reply to Number | AAA
G 818 | 16th | |

1st Army report 8th Liverpool
Regt 51st Div took Salient
L10 L8 K6 aaa Grenadiers
7th Div K6 to J10
aaa Later reports to effect
that 8th Liverpool have been
driven out of Salient L10
L8 K6 aaa as far
as is known Grenadiers still
occupy K6 to J10 aaa
troops that captured J4 to
J2 have been driven back
aaa Efforts tomorrow will be
Concentrated on Northern end of
RUE D'OUVERT aaa 1st Corps
will assist with artillery fire
aaa Details of Cooperation required
will be communicated later

FROM 1st Corps 10.40 pm
PLACE & TIME

War Diary.

47th (London) Division.

Tactical Progress Report
up to Noon, June 13th, 1915.

Operations. I. A few Germans were reported near SHIVERS SOUTH during the night and were fired on by the French Artillery.

Work. II. **W. Section.**

General work on trenches. Grass cut. Trench to French line deepened and traversed. Work carried out on Keeps A, B, C and D.

X. Section.

Damage done by enemy's shells to fire and communication trenches repaired. SAP 19 repaired. Work continued on Keeps E, F, G and H. Wiring of New Posts H is nearly completed.

Information. III. Machine Guns are suspected at the following places :-
M.10.c 1.9 on North side of ruined house. M.10.a 7.2 On Railway Embankment. On North side of Iron Building M.11.a 1.2. On North West side of long single storey building M.4.c 7.0. Large earthworks M.4.a 5.3 at base of North CRASSIER. Large loophole facing South West G.34.c 9.8, where trench crosses road; and possible in advanced trench on North side of Road at G.34.c 5.4. G.54.a 4.6 in haystack on South side of Road facing South.

Trench observed running North from LENS Road at G.35.c 8.1 to 9.6 passing along front of Cemetery then East towards LOOS. It then goes North to G.35.a 9.9 and across Road North as far as about G.29.c 5.4 as shown on Map. This trench is strongly wired, and evidently forms line of defence.

At Cemetery single trench running along South West with High Wire Entanglement in front and low wire fence about 20 yards in front running from G.35.c 5.6 to G.35.a 8.8 was seen.

From G.35.b 5.7 North to Road trench was almost invisible.

At G.29.c 8.1, just North of road, wire appears very strong. From this point trench runs in among a number of haystacks and disappears from sight.

Trench from G.35.a 1.6 to G.23.b 9.9 is not wired.

There appear to be other covered communications along road from G.34.c 5.6 North East to G.35.a 1.6.

Communication trench at G.34.b 2.5 passes under LOOS Road by tunnel which is protected on North West side by earthworks and brushwood screen.

Trench from G.23.c 5.7 to point (1) in G.29.b has a high wire entanglement on its South West side.

1. P. T. O.

From G.22.d 4.9 to G.23.a 8.2 a wire entanglement can be seen behind the German front line.

Trench from G.23.c 8.7 to point (1) in G.23.b has a high wire entanglement on its South West side. The trench crosses the sky line and is lost to view near G.23.c (3).

From G.23.c 0.2 to G.23.c 4.5 and from G.22.d 4.3 to G.23.a 8.2 wire entanglement can be seen in rear of German first line.

It is thought that there is a German strong point around G.23.a 5.0.

Sgd. J.H.R. Hunt Capt.
for. Major General,
Commanding 47th Division.

47th Div. G/31/3
15th June, 1915.

"C" Form (Duplicate). Army Form C. 2123.
MESSAGES AND SIGNALS.   No. of Message.

Service Instructions.   Charges to Pay   Office Stamp
                        £   s.   d.   Y 17.VI.15 L
                                          TELEGRAPH

Handed in at _____ Office 9 5 a.m. Received 9 7 a.m.

TO Hq 6th Div

Sender's Number	Day of Month	In reply to Number	AAA
G823	15		

The 6th Inf Bde is no longer in Corps reserve and is at disposal of 2nd Div aaa 1st Guards Bde remains in Corps reserve and added 1st and aaa 2nd Divns repto 47th Div

H21
9 9 am

FROM   1st Corps
PLACE & TIME 8 50 am

"A" Form.   Army Form C. 2121.
MESSAGES AND SIGNALS.   No. of Message_____

Prefix____ Code____m.	Words	Charge	This message is on a/c of:	Recd. at____m.
Office of Origin and Service Instructions.				Date_____
	Sent			From_____
SECRET	At____m.		_____Service.	
	To____			By_____
	By____		(Signature of "Franking Officer.")	

TO { [As below — Copy to A & Q] }

| Sender's Number | Day of Month | In reply to Number | AAA |
| GR 936 | Seventeenth | | |

Units in Divisional Reserve will remain in readiness to move at one hours notice AAA Headquarters 141st Bde will return to NOEUX LES MINES but the battalion which moved from there to MAZINGARBE last night will remain for the present at MAZINGARBE AAA Addressed 47th Div Mtd Troops, Arty, and Engrs 140th 141st and 142nd Inf Bdes

From   47th Div.
Place
Time   9.30 a.m.

(Z) W. Ruthven Lieut. Col.

"A" Form. Army Form C. 2121.

MESSAGES AND SIGNALS.

TO	140th Inf Brig
	141st Inf Brig
	142nd Inf Brig

Sender's Number	Day of Month	In reply to Number	
G.H 937	17		AAA

The reliefs which were postponed last night may now be carried out under similar arrangements to those made for last night AAA Addressed 140th 141st & 142nd Inf Brigs

From 47th Div
Time 10-10 a.m

H R Hunt Capt G.S

"A" Form.   Army Form C. 2121.

MESSAGES AND SIGNALS.

SECRET

TO [As below]

G.A. 938 Seventeenth   AAA

141st Inf Bde will relieve 142nd
Inf Bde in Section W on the night
of 20/21st under arrangements to
be made between Brigades direct
AAA On completion of the relief
142nd Inf Bde will billet as
follows AAA Two battalions at
MAZINGARBE remainder of Brigade
at NOEUX LES MINES AAA Completion
of relief will be reported AAA
Acknowledge AAA Addressed 47th
Div Mtd Troops Arty Engrs
140th 141st & 142nd Inf Bdes
Train Med A & Q repeated
1st Corps and Adv. 2nd Div.

From: 47th Div.
Place:
Time: 11 a.m.

Signature: W. Ruthven Lieut Col

"C" Form (Duplicate). Army Form C. 2123.
MESSAGES AND SIGNALS. No. of Message

Charges to Pay Office Stamp.
£   s.   d.

Service Instructions. 2 addos
4 2 7

Handed in at ___ Office 12·15 p.m. Received 12·23 p.m.

TO 47th Div

| Sender's Number | Day of Month | In reply to Number | AAA |
| BM 792 | 17 | | |

Operation order No 22 of
15th inst is amended as
follows aaa No 1 line read
2 for June 16/17th read
17/18th aaa No 2 line 2
for June 17/18th read
18/19th aaa the remainder of the
order holds good aaa acknowledge

4·23 p.m.
12·27

FROM 142nd Inf Bde
PLACE & TIME 12·5 P.m.

"C" Form (Duplicate).
MESSAGES AND SIGNALS.

| Handed in at | G.L.E | Office 12.54 p.m. | Received 12.57 p.m. |

TO: 47th Div.

Sender's Number	Day of Month	In reply to Number	AAA
BM 868	17th		

GHQ 938 received aaa Bde HQ established NOEUX-LES-MINES

FROM / PLACE & TIME: 141st Inf Bde 12.48 p.m.

"A" Form.   Army Form C. 2121.

MESSAGES AND SIGNALS. No. of Message_____

Prefix___Code___m.	Words	Charge	This message is on a/c of :	Recd. at___m.
Office of Origin and Service Instructions.	Sent			Date___
	At___m.		___Service.	From___
	To___			
	By___		(Signature of "Franking Officer")	By___

TO { 47th Div Cyclists
     Edwards Horse }   C/ to A.T.O

Sender's Number G.H 939   Day of Month 17   In reply to Number   AAA

Major Hermon King Edwards Horse will take over charge of the Divisional Bombing School with effect from 18-6-15 AAA 47th Div Cyclists will give him any assistance asked for AAA The class now under instruction will remain in its present billets and will return to regimental duty when instruction is completed AAA The next class will assemble at billets to be selected by Major Hermon AAA A programme of instruction proposed for the next class and will be submitted to Div HQ and the proposed billets reported AAA Programme of 1st Class held is attached for information AAA Duration of class may be increased if considered desirable AAA Addressed Edwards Horse repeated 47th Div Cyclists

From 47th Div
Place
Time 3.0 p.m

The above may be forwarded as now corrected. (Z)   H.R. Hunt Capt G.S.
                                    Censor.   Signature of Addresser or person authorised to telegraph in his name

* This line should be erased if not required.
C27642 P. G. Ltd. Wt. W14142/641—20,000 3/15. Forms C2121/10.

"A" Form.   Army Form C. 2121.

MESSAGES AND SIGNALS.   No. of Message_____

Prefix____Code____m. Office of Origin and Service Instructions.	Words	Charge	This message is on a/c of :	Recd. at____m.
	Sent At____m. To____ By____		Service. (Signature of "Franking Officer")	Date____ From____ By____

TO { 140th Inf Brig
      141st Inf Brig
      142nd Inf "   Reply to Q.

Sender's Number	Day of Month	In reply to Number	AAA
G.N 940	17th		

Battalions of 141st Inf Brig usually billeted at NOEUX LES MINES will remain at MAZINGARBE for the present AAA Working parties from Brigades will be detailed tonight as usual AAA Addressed 140th 141st & 142nd Inf Brig

From 47th Div
Place
Time 3 p.m.

The above may be forwarded as now corrected.   (Z)   H.R. Hunt Capt G.S
                          Censor.   Signature of Addresser or person authorised to telegraph in his name

* This line should be erased if not required.

"A" Form. Army Form C. 2121.

MESSAGES AND SIGNALS.

Prefix____ Code____ m.
Office of Origin and Service Instructions.

Secret

TO: 47th Div Arty

Sender's Number: G H 943
Day of Month: 17th
AAA

Should the necessity of moving into position the artillery of the Divn which is now resting be anticipated Special orders will be issued AAA These Units will be in readiness to move at two hours notice and will not be affected by any General orders issued as to the state of readiness of the Divisional Reserve

From: 47th Div
Time: 3-45 p.m.

HR Hunt Capt G.S.

"A" Form.
Army Form C. 2121.

MESSAGES AND SIGNALS.

No. of Message_____

Prefix____Code____m. Office of Origin and Service Instructions.	Words	Charge	This message is on a/c of:	Recd. at____m.
	Sent			Date____
	At____m.		____Service.	From____
	To____			
	By____		(Signature of "Franking Officer")	By____

TO { 140th 142nd Inf. Bde

Sender's Number	Day of Month	In reply to Number	
* G.H.946	17th		AAA

1½ inch Trench Mortar Battery complete with personnel and ammunition will reach your H.Q. tonight for employment in X Section AAA Personnel will be attached to one of the battalions in front line for rations AAA. Four 95 m.m Trench Mortars now in Section X will be transferred to Section W under arrangements to be made direct between Brigades AAA Addressed 140th Inf Bde Repeated 142nd Inf. Bde.

From 47th Div
Place
Time 6-40 pm

The above may be forwarded as now corrected. (Z)

Censor. H.R. Hunt Capt G.S.
Signature of Addressor or person authorised to telegraph in his name

* This line should be erased if not required.
C27642 P.G. Ltd. Wt. W14142/541—20,000 3/15. Forms C2121/10.

"A" Form. Army Form C. 2121.
MESSAGES AND SIGNALS.

Prefix	Code	m.	Words	Charge	This message is on a/c of:	Recd. at	m.
Office of Origin and Service Instructions.						Date	
			Sent At	m.	Service.	From	
			To				
			By		(Signature of "Franking Officer.")	By	

TO { 140th Inf Bde
     141st Inf Bde

Sender's Number	Day of Month	In reply to Number	
GS 948	Seventeenth		AAA

Ref my GS 946 of today AAA Following received from 1st Corps begins AAA Owing to the late arrival of trench mortar battery they will be put up here for the night and sent on in the morning AAA ends

From 47th Div.
Place
Time 8.10 pm

Signature: H.R. Hunt Capt G.S.

"C" Form (Duplicate).　　　　Army Form C. 2123.
MESSAGES AND SIGNALS.　　No. of Message

AR KO 49 Abo
　　　　　　　gns

Service Instructions. Priority

Handed in at Abo　　Office 10.20 p.m.　Received 10.28 p.m.

TO: 47 H Div

Sender's Number: Y831　Day of Month: 17　In reply to Number:　　AAA

Some railway activity was noticed this evening from East towards DON and LENS aaa Take all precautions against hostile counter attacks aaa 1st Gds Bde will be in readiness to move at one hours notice till further orders aaa Acknowledge

452
10.28 p.m.

FROM PLACE & TIME: 1st Corps　10.20 p.m.

G.O.C.

47th (London) Division.

TACTICAL PROGRESS REPORT

up to noon 17th June 1915.

OPERATIONS.
1. Enemy's patrol reached and attempted to cut our front line wire in W2. The patrol was dispersed by rifle fire.
   German aeroplane dropped two large incendiary bombs at 9.35 a.m. on dugouts West of Fosse 7. Bombs were dropped with great accuracy but little damage was done.

WORK.
2. W Section. Work on Keep A continued. General repair and improvement of lines A & B. Work continued on Keeps B, C & D.

   X.1 Section. New communication trench commenced, parapets strengthened and communication trenches 1 & 4 deepened.

   X.2 Section. Repairs and improvements to front line trenches. Work on trench 12 continued.

INFORMATION.
3. About M.10.a.1.0 there is a small gap in the German wire. Wire just N.E. of this point is particularly strong. There is a very large loophole or tunnel in the parapet at M.4.c.6.3. Gap in wire at M.4.a.2.2 has been closed by a single chevaux de frise. Brushwood screen was observed across the LOOS road between the house at G.35.c.4.5. There is a thin line of wire entanglement between G.34.a.5.5 and Sap 18. Head of German sap at G.34.a.8.5 is protected by thin wire entanglement; where this sap starts from German fire trench it is crossed by chevaux de frise. New chevaux de frise have been placed in position at the head of German sap at G.34.a.5.9 South of LENS road. These chevaux de frise are now a formidable obstacle. G.23.d.0.0 appears to be a strong point protected by wire entanglement. German second line appears to be strongly wired near this point – further details required. Machine gun suspected at M.10.a.4.4.

AMENDMENT.
The first para of p.2 of Progress Report dated 16th inst. will be deleted.

H.R. Hunt Capt.

17th June 1915.
G/51/5.

Major General,
Commanding 47th Division.

"A" Form. Army Form C. 2121.

MESSAGES AND SIGNALS.

TO	140th Inf Brig 141st " 142nd " 47 Div Engs

Sender's Number	Day of Month	In reply to Number	AAA
G.H 957	18		

Orders will be issued that in the event of the enemy attacking while working parties from Reserve Battns or the Reserve Brigade are at work these working parties will attach themselves to the nearest Unit AAA They should not attempt to rejoin their Battns after a hostile attack has been launched unless working close to the Battn place of assembly. AAA Addressed 140th 141st 142nd Inf Brig 47th Div Engineers.

From 47th Div
Place
Time 8.59 am.

The above may be forwarded as now corrected. (Z) H.R. Hunt Capt G.S.

"C" Form (Duplicate).
MESSAGES AND SIGNALS.

Army Form C. 2123.

No. of Message

Am Egl 3b abo Jones

Charges to Pay. £ s. d.

Office Stamp. 16 VI 15 LB TELEGRAPHS

Service Instructions.

Handed in at Abo Office 5.37 p.m. Received 5.40 p.m.

TO 4th Div

Sender's Number	Day of Month	In reply to Number	AAA
G 48	18		

When reporting gun flashes seen at night the exact time should when possible be reported aaa this assists checking by cross bearings in many cases

96a   470   5.25 pm
            5.1

FROM PLACE & TIME First Corps 5.10 pm

Wt.W.9668—1672. 50,000 Pads. 1584—1/15. S. B. Ltd.—Forms/C.2123.

War Diary

47th (London) Division.

Tactical Progress Report
up to Noon, June 18th 1915.

Operations.   I.   Enemy opened rapid fire at about 2.15 a.m. for no reason, opposite W.3.

Work.   II.   W. Section.

Work continued on Keep A and trench to French line. Trenches repaired and improved.

X. Section.

New wire between Saps 13 and 14 completed. Sixty yards of wire erected from Sap 13 towards Sap 12. 200 yards of French wire put out on new front line.
Work continued on Posts E and F.

Information.   III.   At M.10.a 3.2 a sap 20 yards long, protected by Chevaux de frise, runs Westwards.

Trench from M.10.a 6.3 to main building of Puits No. 16 is protected by entanglement 4' high and 6' to 8' wide.

Signs of fresh digging were seen in Trench at M.4.c 6.9.

Wall on West side of PUITS No. 11 is loopholed.

Chalk Pit at about M.6.a 9.3 appears to be connected by a trench or sunken road to bushes at M.6.c 8.8.

Strong point suspected at M.6.c 3.7 on LENS road.

Brushwood screen at G.35.c 7.1 has been enlarged and the trench here appears stronger.

Wire at salients (3) and (1) in G.28.b is an entanglement 5' high and 6' wide strengthened by chevaux de frise and is very strong.

Sap running out from G.23.a 4.0 to (3) is strongly wired and has loopholes at the sap head.

Trench from G.22.b (1) to G.23.a (3) appears to be unused and is in bad repair.

Machine guns suspected at G.28.b 3.7 and G.22.d (2).

47th Div.G/51/5

18th June 1915

H.R. Strutt Capt
for Major General,
Commanding 47th Division.

"C" Form (Duplicate).
MESSAGES AND SIGNALS.

Army Form C. 2123.

No. of Message

			Charges to Pay		Office Stamp.
HR	6	ACO	2	d.	
		Campten	s.		

Service Instructions.

Handed in at ACO Office 7.21 a.m. Received _____ m.

TO 47 Div

Sender's Number	Day of Month	In reply to Number	
G 849	19th		AAA

Aircraft report unusual railway activity at LABASSEE at 4 am and at DON at 5 am aaa Have all reserves in readiness to deal with hostile counter-attack aaa 1st Guards bde ready to move at one hours notice aaa addsd 1st 2nd and 47th Divs and Aeronautics 3

8.35 am
CR.97

FROM
PLACE & TIME   1st Corps 8.20 am

Wt.W.9668—1672. 50,000 Pads. 1584—1/15. S. B. Ltd.—Forms/C.2123.

"A" Form. Army Form C. 2121.
MESSAGES AND SIGNALS.   No. of Message_____

Prefix	Code	m.	Words	Charge	This message is on a/c of:	Recd. at	m.
Office of Origin and Service Instructions.			Sent			Date	
			At	m.	Service.	From	
			To			By	
			By		(Signature of "Franking Officer.")		

TO { 47th Div. Arty. 140th 141st
    and 142nd Inf Bdes

Sender's Number | Day of Month | In reply to Number | AAA
G.R.973 | Nineteenth | |

Following from 1st Corps begins AAA Aircraft report unusual railway activity at LA BASSEE at 4 am. and at DON at 5 a.m. AAA Have all reserves in readiness to deal with hostile counter-attack AAA 1st Guards Bde ready to move at one hours notice AAA ends AAA Reserves *except artillery* should be prepared to leave their billets at short notice AAA Addressed 47th Div. Arty 140th 141st and 142nd Inf Bdes

From 47th Div.
Place
Time 8.45 a.m.

"C" Form (Duplicate).
MESSAGES AND SIGNALS. Army Form C. 2123.

Sm Db, 53 Abo

Handed in at Abo Office 4.07 m. Received m.

TO 47th Divn

Sender's Number	Day of Month	In reply to Number	AAA
G852	19		

Two 15 pounder Batteries will move into position night 20th–21st inst to be attached 2nd Divn AAA one Battery will be attached to 41st Bde and one to 36th Bde AAA details to be arranged between Divisions AAA 47th Divn lefts 2nd Divn

4.58
4.13 p

FROM 1st Corps
PLACE & TIME 4.07 pm

"A" Form.   Army Form C. 2121.

MESSAGES AND SIGNALS.

No. of Message _____

Prefix ____ Code ____ m.	Words	Charge	This message is on a/c of:	Recd. at ____ m.
Office of Origin and Service Instructions.	Sent			Date ____
____	At ____ m.		____ Service.	From ____
____	To ____			By ____
____	By ____		(Signature of "Franking Officer.")	

TO {
47th Div Arty		47th Div Engrs	
140th,	141st	and	142nd
Inf	Bdes		
}

Sender's Number	Day of Month	In reply to Number	
G.R.980	Nineteenth		AAA

| The G.O.C. would like to see you at the Chateau at |
| MAZINGARBE at 9 p.m. tonight |

| ADDED to | 141st – | G.O.C. will pick you up as he passes |
| | | your house on his way to the Chateau. |

| ADDED to | 142nd – | Motor will call for you at 8.45 p.m. |

From: 47th Div
Place:
Time: 7.45 p.m.

The above may be forwarded as now corrected. (Z)
(Sd) H.R.HUNT Capt. G.S.
Censor.   Signature of Addressor or person authorised to telegraph in his name.

"A" Form. Army Form C. 2121.
MESSAGES AND SIGNALS.

TO	140th Inf. Bde		
	141st Inf. Bde		addomg
	142nd Inf. Bde		

Sender's Number: G.H.983 Day of Month: 19th AAA

Relief of Section "W" arranged for night of 20th/21st are postponed and will be carried out during night of 21st/22nd June. AAA Acknowledge. AAA Addressed 141st and 142nd Inf. Bde. Repeated 140th Inf. Bde.

From 47th Div
Time 10-15 pm

H.R. Hunt Capt G.S.

47th (London) Division.
47th Div. G/51/5
19th June 1915.

Tactical Progress Report
up to Noon, June 19th, 1915.

Operations.   I.   Enemy fired 48 15-Centimetre H. E. shells from the direction of VIOLAINES on the area just West of FOSSE No. 7 at about 4 p.m. 19.6.15.

Work.   II. **Section W.**

General work on front trenches. Work on trench to French line and on Keeps continued.

Section X.

Sapping continued from Sap 15 to 16.
Single width of wire completed from Sap 14 to Sap 15.
Posts G and H continued.
Erection of overhead cover on Trench 12 continued.
Trenches 2, 9, 14 and 16 deepened and fire steps provided.

Information.   III.   Strong point at G.28.d is wired on South and West sides, other two faces are not visible.

German Second Line Trench is wired from G.34.a 8.6 to G.28.d 0.3 where wire disappears from sight.

Wire from M.10.a 4.4 to M.4.c 4.0 appears to have been strengthened and is about 15 feet wide at M.4.c 4.9.

Wire at M.4.a 6.4 has been strengthened by six chevaux de frise.

MAROC - LOOS Road is barricaded at G.34.d 0.7 and again with carts at G.34.b 4.1.

Wire on line G.28.b (3) - (1) has been strengthened by chevaux de frise at intervals.

Machine Gun Emplacements suspected at G.28.b 3.6, G.28.b 3.7, G.28.b 3.8 and at point of salient G.28.b 2.9

Five German Observation Balloons were in the air at 3 p.m. to-day. One in the direction of CITE ST. ELIE, one at LOOS, one South of LOOS and two in the direction of LENS. These latter two were reported to be about twice as far from our lines as the others.

for Major General,
Commanding 47th Division.

"A" Form.
MESSAGES AND SIGNALS.
Army Form C. 2121.

Prefix	Code	m.	Words	Charge	This message is on a/c of:	Recd. at	m.
Office of Origin and Service Instructions.			Sent			Date	
			At	m.	Service.	From	
			To			By	
			By		(Signature of "Franking Officer.")		

TO { 47 Div Arty   47 Div Engs
     140. 141.   142 Inf Bde

Sender's Number	Day of Month	In reply to Number	AAA

GH 986 Twentieth

GOC RA, CRE and GOC.
Inf Bdes will meet Major
General Commanding at 4 pm
today at Chateau MAZINGARBE

From 47th Div
Place
Time 1 pm

"A" Form.
Army Form C. 2121.
MESSAGES AND SIGNALS. No. of Message _____

Prefix ____ Code ____ m.	Words	Charge	This message is on a/c of:	Recd. at ____ m.
Office of Origin and Service Instructions.				Date ____
~~SECRET~~	Sent At ____ m.		_____ Service.	From ____
	To ____			By ____
	By ____		(Signature of "Franking Officer.")	

TO	140th	141st	142nd	Inf. Bde.

Sender's Number	Day of Month		In reply to Number	A A A
* G.W.991	29th			

Reference	my	G.H.983	of	19th	June
AAA	Reliefs	in	Section	"W"
will	be	carried	out	tonight
as	originally	ordered	AAA	Acknowledge
AAA	Addressed	140th	141st	and
142nd	Inf. Bdes.			

From 47th Div.
Place
Time 6 p.m.

The above may be forwarded as now corrected. (Z)
Censor.   Signature of Addressor or person authorised to telegraph in his name.

M Webber
Capt.

* This line should be erased if not required.

"A" Form.				Army Form C. 2121.
MESSAGES AND SIGNALS.				No. of Message_____
Prefix_____Code_____m. Office of Origin and Service Instructions.	Words | Charge Sent At_____m. To_____ By_____	This message is on a/c of: _____Service. (Signature of "Franking Officer")		Recd. at_____m. Date_____ From_____ By_____

TO: Edwards Horse
141st Inf Brig.

Sender's Number	Day of Month	In reply to Number	AAA
* G.H 992	20		

Troops of King Edwards horse will be attached in rotation to 141st Inf Brig for a tour of 48 hours in trenches AAA Attachment of first troop will commence evening Tuesday 22nd AAA Arrangements will be made between 141st Inf Brig and Edwards Horse direct AAA Addressed Edwards Horse 141st Inf Brig

From 47th Div
Place
Time 6-35 p.m

The above may be forwarded as now corrected. (Z) H.R. Hunt Capt G.S
Censor. Signature of Addresser or person authorised to telegraph in his name

* This line should be erased if not required.

47th Div.G/51/5.
20th June 1915.

47th (LONDON) DIVISION.

TACTICAL PROGRESS REPORT
up to Noon, June 20th, 1915.

Operations 1. Nil.

Work. 2. Section W.
Keeps. Work continued on trench to French Line and on General repairs to trenches.

Section X.
160 yards of wire single width erected between Saps 12 and 13. 60 yards of fire trench, average 3 ft deep, dug between Saps 14 and 15.
Work on Posts G and H, and on Trench 12, continued. Sap 18 improved.

Information.3. The cigar shaped Observation Balloon which is over DOUVRIN is reported to be wired to a point, true bearing 48 degrees from northern edge of FOSSE No.7. The balloon rose from behind some trees West of DOUVRIN.

Signalling was observed from the Tower of FOSSE No.13 and was answered from LA BASSEE.

Patrols report enemy's wire opposite W.1 Section to be weak and that there are gaps in it from 10 to 20 feet wide.

From the double Crassier towards M.5.c.7.8. there is a continuous trench to about M.5.c.4.6., where a Machine Gun emplacement is suspected.

No wire can be seen along this trench.

Communication trench from M.5.c.2.5. leads up the northern side of the ~~crassier~~ double crassier.

Trench from M.5.c.2.5. to PUITS No.11 runs up hill and is well traversed.

The Chalk Pit at M.6.a.9.3. appears to have a parapet along its western edge.

Wire between G.34.a.5.8. and G.28.c.7.1. appears to have been further strengthened by chevaux de frise. A working party was heard here on night of 18th.

opposite/ From G.28.b.4.1 to Sap 12, the German line consists of an ordinary trench with wire about 4 ft high and 5 to 6 ft wide. At frequent intervals the parapet appears to be strengthened and the wire is thicker at these points, which are possibly M.G. Emplacements.

At.G.28.b.4.2. there are two such points which jut a short distance in front of the main trench. At about M.28.b.3.5 there is a strong sand bag emplacement. The wire here is 6 ft high and 10 ft wide. Just north of this point wire is not so strong, but becomes very strong again at M.28.b.2.8. where there are two of these emplacements and is about 18 ft wide at this point.

At the apex of the salient in G.28.b. there is a Sap running out for a short distance Northwards in the wire entanglement, which is very thick at this point and about 6 ft high.

There is a tunnel in the barricade at G.34.d.0.7. mentioned in yesterday's progress report. A trench or ditch from the fire trench passes along the north of the road and through the barricade by means of this tunnel.

No wire was detected behind the German front line from G.28.b.4.1. to opposite Sap 12, except at G.28.b.3.8. where a few chevaux de frise were seen, which might only be for strengthening front wire in case of need.

Captain,
for Major General,
Commanding 47th (Lon) Division.

"A" Form. Army Form C. 2121.

MESSAGES AND SIGNALS. No. of Message_____

Prefix_____Code_____m.	Words	Charge	This message is on a/c of:	Recd. at_____m.
Office of Origin and Service Instructions.				Date_____
_____	Sent		_____Service.	From_____
_____	At_____m.			
_____	To_____			
_____	By_____		(Signature of "Franking Officer.")	By_____

TO { First Corps

| Sender's Number | Day of Month | In reply to Number | AAA |

* GW 997 Twentyfirst
Relief of W Section complete
command of Section taken over by
141st Iny Bde aaa W1 18th
Bn W2 20th Bn W3 19th Bde Res
17th Bn aaa

From 47th Div
Place
Time 1. am.

The above may be forwarded as now corrected.   (Z)

Censor.   Signature of Addressor or person authorised to tele[graph]

* This line should be erased if not required.

"C" Form (Duplicate).
MESSAGES AND SIGNALS.

Army Form C. 2123

No. of Message

Charges to Pay.
£   s.   d.

Office Stamp.
21.VI.15
TELEGRAPHS

Service Instructions.

Handed in at _____ Office _____ m. Received _____ m.

TO 4th Div

Sender's Number	Day of Month	In reply to Number	AAA
baby	21		
12	large	high explosive	shells
have	just	been fired	in
rapid	succession	over	village west
FOSSE 7	from	direction of	AUCHY
or	HAISNE	and	have informed
artillery		524	
		L.O anti	

FROM PLACE & TIME

W.9668/1672. 50,000 Pads. 12/14. A.W. & Co. Forms/C.2193.

"C" Form (Duplicate).   Army Form C. 2123
MESSAGES AND SIGNALS.   No. of Message............

| | Charges to Pay. £ s. d. | Office Stamp. Y 21 VI 15 LB TELEGRAPHS |

Service Instructions.

Handed in at **3rd** Office **10.29** m. Received **10.31** m.

TO **47th Div**

Sender's Number	Day of Month	In reply to Number	AAA
BM/763	21st	GA 775	

attachment of 15th and 16th LON BATTERIES to 2nd DIV now completed aaa

5.32
10.40 am

FROM **47th Div Arty**
PLACE & TIME **10-25 am**

W 9668/1672. 50,000 Pads. 12/14 A. W. & Co. Forms/C.2123.

"C" Form (Duplicate). Army Form C. 2123

MESSAGES AND SIGNALS.

No. of Message ....

Charges to Pay Office Stamp.
£ s. d.

Service Instructions:

Handed in at .... Office .... m. Received .... m.

TO 47 Div

Sender's Number	Day of Month	In reply to Number	AAA
1676	21		

Enemy have shelled LE PHILOSOPHE for three hours doing considerable damage to existing houses aaa Sixth Battn Hq has been completely demolished and a large quantity of stores kits and officers mess goods have been completely buried aaa Artillery informed aaa.

FROM 140 Inf Bde
PLACE & TIME 6.30 pm

"A" Form. Army Form C. 2121.

MESSAGES AND SIGNALS.

Prefix ___ Code ___ m.	Words	Charge	This message is on a/c of:	Recd. at ___ m.
Office of Origin and Service Instructions.	Sent			Date ___
	At ___ m.		___ Service	From ___
	To ___			
	By ___		(Signature of "Franking Officer")	By ___

TO 142 BDE
    47 DIV MTD TROOPS
    47 DIV ARTY

| Sender's Number | Day of Month | In reply to Number | AAA |
| GW 8 | 21 | | |

The Infantry Brigade in Divisional
Reserve and Div MTD Troops
will be in readiness to
move at two hours notice
AAA Artillery Units at three
hours notice AAA Addressed 142
Bde Div MTD Troops and
Div Arty.

From 47th DIVN
Place
Time 7.20 pm

Signature: W Webbe ?

"C" Form (Original).
MESSAGES AND SIGNALS.

Army Form C. 2123.

Prefix	Code	Words	Received From	Sent, or sent out	Office Stamp
Charges to collect £ s. d.			By Thos	At ... m. To ... By	21.VII.15 LB TELEGRAPHS
Service Instructions.					

Handed in at 2hrs   Office 11.40 p.m.   Received 11.50 p.

TO 47 Divn

*Sender's Number	Day of Month	In reply to Number	AAA
M69215	21		

Heavy shelling by french batteries commenced at 11·6 pm aaa Since ascertained that 4 french batteries are each firing 150 incendiary shells into L.005 aaa all quiet on our front

569
11.55 pm

FROM 140 Inf Bde
PLACE & TIME 11·40 pm

War Diary

47th Div. G/51/5
21st June 1915.

47th (London) Division.

Tactical Progress Report
up to Noon June 21st 1915.

Operations.   I.   12 large High Explosive Shells were fired in rapid succession over village at FOSSE No. 7 from direction of AUCHY at about 1.20 a.m.

Enemy working party in front of FOSSE No. 16 dispersed by rifle fire.

Work.   II.   **W. Section.**

Communication Trenches improved. General repairs to front line. Grass cutting begun.

X. Section.

75 yards fire trench average depth 2'6" dug between SAPS 14 and 15. Wiring between Saps 13 and 12½ almost completed. Fire trenches traversed and repaired. Communication trenches deepened. Roofing of Trench 12 completed.

Information.   III.   There is a short length of trench just in front of a house at about M.11.a 3.7.

Houses at M.11.a 4.8 are connected by a wooden barricade.

A wooden barricade runs across the mine enclosure at PUITS No. 11 from South West to North East, just in front of the Pit Head.

There is a 20-foot gap in the wire from the DOUBLE CRASSIER at M.5.c 4.1 to M.6.c 4.6 at the point where it crosses the road to PUITS No. 11. No trench can be seen behind this wire except for a short length North of a house at about M.5.D 5.3. This wire runs closer to the railway than is shown on tracing.

From M.6.c 3.7 a wired trench runs West of the house at this point, crosses the LENS road at M.6.c 2.8 about 50 yards North of a house on the East side of the road and runs along the North edge of scrub bushes for 30 or 40 yards, thence curves round West of the LOOS - CITE ST. EDOUARD road, through about the North East angle of M.5.b. It passes through G.35.c 9.6 at G.35.c 8.3. trench from M.5.a 1.6 to G.35.c 9.6 at G.35.c 8.3.

The wire appears to be an entanglement about 4 feet high and 6 feet to 8 feet wide. From the house at M.6.c 3.7 the wire runs due South over the ridge and is lost to sight. Where it crosses the ridge the wire

/appears

appears broader and stronger than it is further North.

A wire obstacle is visible at the side of LENS road at M.6.c 1.8 ready to be put in position to block the road.

A trench runs from the house on the East side of the road along the edge of the road up to the entanglement and ends in what appears to be a short length of Fire trench or Machine Gun Emplacement.

The houses on LENS road and the point at which the trench crosses the road at G.35.d 2.4 appear to be strong points.

At M.4.a 8.9 where the front line trench bends East, a line of wire continues North as far as G.34.c 8.2. Here it turns East and rejoins the entanglement in front of the trench, thus forming a sort of rectangle.

In this rectangle is a crater, probably a listening post.

From M.4.a 8.9 to G.34.c 8.1 this front line of wire is high wire entanglement, from G.34.c 8.1 to G.34.c 8.2 low wire about 2 feet high, and from G.34.c 8.2 to G.34.d 1.3 it is again high wire.

Enemy heard adding to wire in front of M.4.a 2.2 during night of 20th/21st instant.

Signal lights apparently receiving messages from South observed on a true bearing of 37 degrees from M.3.a 8.5 between 11.30 p.m. 20th and 2 a.m. 21st.

Large fire in enemy's lines apparently South end of HULLUCH believed to be caused by our shells, reported 6.25 p.m. 21/6/15.

J.R. Hunter Capr
for Major General,
Commanding 47th Division.

appears broader and stronger than it is further North.

A wire obstacle is visible at the side of LENS road at M.6.c 1.8 ready to be put in position to block the road.

A trench runs from the house on the East side of the road along the edge of the road up to the entanglement and ends in what appears to be a short length of Fire trench or Machine Gun Emplacement.

The houses on LENS road and the point at which the trench crosses the road at G.35.d 2.4 appear to be strong points.

At M.4.a 8.9 where the front line trench bends East, a line of wire continues North as far as G.34.c 8.2. Here it turns East and rejoins the entanglement in front of the trench, thus forming a sort of rectangle.

In this rectangle is a crater, probably a listening post.

From M.4.a 8.9 to G.34.c 8.1 this front line of wire is high wire entanglement, from G.34.c 8.1 to G.34.c 8.2 low wire about 2 feet high, and from G.34.c 8.2 to G.34.d 1.3 it is again high wire.

Enemy heard adding to wire in front of M.4.a 2.2 during night of 20th/21st instant.

Signal light apparently receiving messages from South observed on a true bearing of 37 degrees from M.3.a 8.5 between 11.30 p.m. 20th and 2 a.m. 21st.

Large fire in enemy's lines apparently South end of HULLUCH believed to be caused by our shells, reported 6.25 p.m. 21/6/15.

J.R. Hunt Capt
for Major General,
Commanding 47th Division.

"C" Form (Duplicate).
MESSAGES AND SIGNALS. Army Form C.2123

Sw aa B	32. Rom	Charges to Pay. £ s. d.	Office Stamp. TELEGRAPH
Service Instructions.			
Handed in at 7/16	Office 15a m.	Received 1.23 m.	

TO 47th Divn

Sender's Number	Day of Month	In reply to Number	AAA
PM 941	22nd		

French artillery began bombarding LOOS 11.10 pm aaa Enemy started replying with heavy shells on LES BREBIS about 11.45 pm aaa Some casualties to 17th Bn billetted in Village aaa near Bde Hq aaa observing officer W2 Reports 12.18 am begins aaa following notion on Bombardment of LOOS five fires started three fair size two of which appeared to be buildings aaa ends

(three fair)

35¼
1.30 a

FROM 141 Inf Bde
PLACE & TIME 12.40 am

W.9668/1672. 50,000 Pads. 12/14. A.W. & Co. Forms/C.2193.

"C" Form (Duplicate).   Army Form C. 2123
MESSAGES AND SIGNALS.

TO 47th Divn

Sender's Number BM3442   **Day of Month** 22   **In reply to Number**   AAA

My 8th Batt AAA casualties 17th
for Regt AAA other ranks
killed four wounded twenty suffering
from shock twentysix AAA 17th
Bn and Bde HQ now
in cellars

FROM 141st Inf Bde
PLACE & TIME 1.44 am

"C" Form (Duplicate).
MESSAGES AND SIGNALS.   No. of Message ....

Army Form C. 2123

			Charges to Pay. £ s. d.	Office Stamp.

Service Instructions.

Handed in at _LLE_ Office _4.55_ m. Received _5.5_ m.

TO _47th Div._

Sender's Number	Day of Month	In reply to Number	AAA
BM 9/44	22		

Situation own what of WI
shelled during night bar some
shells dropped into LES BREBIS
during night own all quiet
new own adv 47th Div
deficated 140th bar 18th Bde
armée francaise

55?
5.10 am

FROM _141 Inf Bde._
PLACE & TIME _4.50 am_

W.9668/1679. 50,000 Pads. 12/14 A. W. & Co. Forms/C.2123.

47th (London) Division.

Tactical Progress Report.
up to Noon, 22nd June, 1915.

47th Division.
G/51/5
22nd June 1915.

Operations. I. PHILOSOPHE shelled during afternoon of 21st by 5.9" guns from the direction of AUCHY-LEZ-LA-BASSEE.

French Artillery fired incendiary shells into LOOS at 11 p.m. and caused five fires.

LES BREBIS shelled by Germans with 11.5 c.m. guns at 11.45 p.m..

Wiring party in W.1 was disturbed last night by light high velocity shells. Our Artillery silenced those guns.

Work. II. W. Section.

General repairs to trenches and wire. Grass cutting continued.
Sap No. 1 deepened.
Saps Nos. 4 and 5 made ready for wiring.
Position for two Sections enfilading front of CRASSIER No. 5 strengthened.
Work on B Line continued.
Communication trenches improved.
Work continued on Keeps A and C and on new communication trench to B line.

X. Section.

65 yards fire trench dug between Saps 14 and 15, average depth 2'6".
30 feet of fire trench dug between Saps 15 and 16.
60 yards of wire put up between Saps 12 and 11.
Additional overhead cover made to trench 12.
Work continued on Posts G. and H.
Front trenches strengthened, new traverses and fire steps made.

Information. III. A trench connects M.4.b 9.2 with the Double CRASSIER at M.4.d 7.8. This trench is wired with a 15 feet gap at base of Crassier..

House at M.5.d 7.3 is probably defended as earthworks can be seen just North of it.

At this point a siding runs out from the railway in a North Easterly direction ending in a high mound of earth at M.5.d 9.4.

No wire has been detected behind German front line near salient in G.28.b.

This salient appears to be correctly shown on AUCHY-LENS trench map 1st Edition and is much blunter than shown in HAISNES Second Edition.

The light coloured lines meeting at G.28.b 1.9 are wired saps. The wire appears to be low wire entanglement and looks old and not in first class condition.

/These

These Saps are only used by sharpshooters. Our line at this point is about 180 yards from the German main line.

Enemy's transport was reported very active on LENS road at 3 a.m., direction of movement towards LENS.

The usual movement of transport was heard on roads near LOOS but ceased as soon as French Artillery bombarded LOOS.

Enemy displayed more activity than usual opposite W. Section.

Opposite W.1 Section trip wire is reported 40 yards in front of the entanglement of the German trench.

Stakes were being driven in behind the German line opposite this Section.

Enemy have erected new high wire entanglement about 150 yards North of FOSSE 16 de LENS on top of the Slag heap running North East from FOSSE.

North of the DOUBLE CRASSIER large enemy working parties were erecting a second line of wire 30 yards in front of the first line which is 20 yards from the trench.

A party of about 40 men was working on the enemy's wire South of the CRASSIER.

Enemy was cutting grass in front of Sap No. 4 in W.2 Section.

There is barley 3'6" high between our lines and the German lines opposite W.2.

Machine gun emplacements are suspected at Base of Sap M.4.c 6.5 and M.4.d 8.9.

Enemy's gun is suspected at M.4.a 8.7 and a Battery on a true bearing of 107 degrees from G.33.d 6.3 and another at G.12.a 8.8 firing from in front of a small wood running from East to West.

The following were observed from FOSSE No. 7 :-

(a) A fixed green light on a true bearing of $22\frac{1}{2}°$.

(b) Battery of heavy guns firing South West from 9 p.m. to 11 p.m. on a true bearing of $131\frac{1}{2}°$. Time between flash and report 18 seconds.

(c) Battery of smaller guns true bearing $124\frac{1}{2}°$.

(d) Three furnaces reported in use on a bearing of $64\frac{1}{2}°$.

for Major General,

Commanding 47th Division.

"C" Form (Duplicate).
Army Form C. 2123.
MESSAGES AND SIGNALS. No. of Message

B G 29 aca
Cunningham

Charges to Pay. £ s. d.

Office Stamp. 23.VI.16 LB

Service Instructions. Priority

Handed in at aca Office 7.0 p.m. Received 7.3 p.m.

TO 47th Div'n

Sender's Number	Day of Month	In reply to Number	AAA
G 918	23rd		

In para 3 of 1st Corps operation order No 89 for Sections Y and Z read Section Z aaa acknowledge

(SW 37)

FROM PLACE & TIME   1st Corps 7 pm

47th Div.No.G/51/5.
23rd June 1915.

47th (LONDON) DIVISION.

TACTICAL PROGRESS REPORT

up to noon 23rd June 1915.

OPERATIONS   1.   --- Nil ---

WORK   2.   "W" Section.

        Fire trench deepened, fire steps constructed, wire repaired and parapets improved.

        Sap 1 deepened and improved.

        Trench to French second line now nearly complete. Usable throughout but requires more fire stopping and traversing.

        Work continued on B line.

"X" Section.

        From Sap 12 to 11, 90 yards of wire have been erected and pickets driven for a further 40 yards.

        Saps 14 and 15 now connected by a traversed fire trench - average depth 3 feet.

        Between Saps 15 and 16, 30 feet of fire trench have been added.

        Work continued on Posts F, G and H.

INFORMATION   3.   At the Salient in M.9.d is a strong entanglement 10' wide; at M.9.d.8.4 the wire continues about 100 yards South forming an advanced line.

        From M.9.d.8.2 to M.9.d.8.3 is a line of very large chevaux de frise.

        On the South side of Sap M.9.d.6.1 as far as the saphead are chevaux de frise, continued for about 100 yards by an ordinary wire entanglement.

        The wall on the West side of the Mine building at PUITS No 16 appears to be loopholed but no wire can be observed in front.

        The Second line trench from M.10.b.0.3 to the North East runs to M.4.d.8.2 and not as previously reported. From M.4.d.8.2 it continues to the double CRASSIER at M.5.c.0.4. Where it crosses the road at the foot of the CRASSIER the parapet has been raised recently and now forms a sandbag breastwork about 8' high. There appears to be a gap in the wire at this point closed by chevaux de frise.

/From

INFORMATION
(continued)

From M.10.b.0.3 to the South West the trench continues across the embankment and is lost to sight about M.10.a.8.2. The trench is wired throughout its whole length as far as the CRASSIER. The wire passes up the side and across the top of the CRASSIER itself. No trench over the CRASSIER has yet been observed at this point.

High velocity gun located on true bearing of 77° from G.33.d.8.3 firing apparently from behind White House North of SIEGE No.15.

Flares sent up last night from FOSSE No 16.

Signal lamp visible about M.10.b.7.3. This lamp is NOT visible from our front line trenches.

Germans reported driving in stakes near M.4.a.1.3 but ceased when a shot was fired from our line G.33.d.

Patrol from Sap 8 reported Germans working North and South of G.34.c.6.8 at 1 a.m. but retired before return of patrol.

A.R. Hunt Capt
for Major General,
Commanding 47th (London) Division.

"C" Form (Duplicate).
MESSAGES AND SIGNALS.

Army Form C. 2123

No. of Message

SB AGW pm 34

Charges to Pay. £ s. d.

Office Stamp.
-Y 24.VI.15 LB

Service Instructions: Priority 10/2 adds

Handed in at ELE   Office 1.38 p.m.   Received 1.45 p.m.

TO 47th Divn

Sender's Number	Day of Month	In reply to Number	
BM 999	24th		AAA

NORTH MAROC and two towards GRENAY being shelled from direction of LENS aaa Size of shells unknown aaa Addressed 47th Div repeated 47th Div arty

6"
1-50 pm

FROM 141st Inf Bde
PLACE & TIME 1.33 pm

"C" Form (Duplicate). Army Form C. 2123
MESSAGES AND SIGNALS. No. of Message...........

Charges to Pay. | Office Stamp.
£   s.   d.

Service Instructions. Priority

Handed in at ZLE Office 2·0 p.m. Received ...... p.m.

TO 47th Div

Sender's Number	Day of Month	In reply to Number	AAA
S6724	24th		

LES BREBIS is being shelled aaa Divisional arty informed

FROM 141st Inf Bde
PLACE & TIME 2 pm

War Diary

47th (London) Division.   47th Div. G/51/5
                                        June 24th 1915.

Tactical Progress Report
up to Noon, June 24th 1915.

Operations.   I.   Enemy fired rifle grenades on to right of Section
                   W.1. We replied effectively with Trench Mortar and
                   rifle grenades.

                   Enemy shelled LES BREBIS and MAROC about 1 p.m.
                   today but ceased fire immediately our counter
                   batteries opened.

Work.   II. W. Section.
                   Wire and parapets repaired.

                   Making fire positions and deepening No. 1 Trench.

                   New trench on left of Section continued, 100 yards
                   new wiring in front.

                   X. Section.

                   Fire trench Sap 14 to Sap 15 improved.

                   Wiring completed between Saps 12 and 11, single
                   width.

                   Work continued on Posts F. G. and H. and
                   satisfactory progress made.

                   Trench No. 12 worked on during day.

                   Communication trench No. 2 deepened and repaired
                   for 30 yards to Eastward of Support Shelter.

Information. III. M.10.a 3.4 appears to be a strong point for flanking
                   defence reached by a trench from M.10.a 5.4.

                   Trench to M.9.b 9.1 appears to be disused, the wire
                   in front of it is a double line of wire, chevaux de
                   frise and trip wire in first line with an entanglement
                   4 feet high and 5 feet wide behind.

                   From M.10.a 5.6 to M.10.a 5.7 there is wire behind
                   front line trench. This wire is not in good condition.

                   Wire across Sap at M.10.a 5.6 appears to have been
                   strengthened.

                   The wire in front of Saphead at M.4.c 2.4 continues
                   North for about 30 yards and is about 4 feet high and
                   4 feet wide.

                   Except for a short T piece at Saphead, no trench
                   leading to M.4.c 2.8 can be seen.

                                                           /There

Information. There are signs of recent digging in trench at M.4.c 5.9.
(Continued)
The line of stakes, apparently for a new line of wire, in front of the DOUBLE CRASSIER has been increased and now reaches to M.4.a 3.4. Wiring has been continued and reaches to M.4.a 1.3.

Wire in front of small salient at G.34.a 6.5 has recently been strengthened.

Suspected Artillery Observing Station located in Fosse 16, two wires attached.

N.W.Webber Capt
for Major General,
Commanding 47th Division.

"C" Form (Duplicate).		Army Form C. 2123
MESSAGES AND SIGNALS.		No. of Message

AyS 32 aeo	Charges to Pay. £ s. d.	Office Stamp. 25.VI.15 LB

Service Instructions.

Handed in at 1st Divn   Office 8.37 a.m.   Received 8.25 a.m.

TO   47th Divn

Sender's Number	Day of Month	In reply to Number	AAA
G456	25/6		
1st	Divnl	headqrs	opens at
MARLES	LES	MINES	at 2.0
pm	today	aaa	addsd 1st
Corps	reptd	2nd	Divn 47th
Divn	9th	Divn	
			628
			8.30

FROM PLACE & TIME   1st Division 8.30 am

W.9668/1672. 50,000 Pads. 12/14. A. W. & Co. Forms/C.2123.

"C" Form (Duplicate). Army Form C. 2123.
MESSAGES AND SIGNALS.
No. of Message

2m XXX 32 A6O Hills

Service Instructions.

Charges to Pay. £ s. d.

Office Stamp.

Handed in at A6O Office 10.50 p.m. Received 10.5? p.m.

TO 47 Div

Sender's Number: 9959
Day of Month: 25
In reply to Number:
AAA

Reference my G957 conference will take place at same place at 3 pm tomorrow instead of time ordered in former wire aaa Acknowledge

6-2
11.0 pm

FROM
PLACE & TIME
1st Corps
10.50 pm

War Diary.

47th Div.No.51/5.
25th June 1915.

47th (LONDON) DIVISION.

TACTICAL PROGRESS REPORT

up to noon 25th June 1915.

OPERATIONS. 1.   Machine gun in W.2 Section opened fire last night on a German working party about M.3.b.9.2 and caused work to stop.

WORK. 2. "W" Section.   General improvement of trenches and wire.
Work continued on Keeps B and D.

"X" Section.   15 yards fire trench dug between Saps 15 & 16.
Improvement of fire trench between Saps 14 & 15 continued.
150 yards of wire single width erected between Saps 11 & 10.
Post E partially wired and work continued on F, G and H.
Work continued on trench 12.
Trench 2 deepened and repaired.

INFORMATION. 3.   At M.4.a.6.4 about 30 feet of wire and stakes have been removed leaving only front and back row of stakes with three or four strands of wire. The parapet here is low and this is probably a starting point for patrols, as it cannot be seen from our front line trenches.

Between G.34.a.7.1 and G.34.a.8.3 parapet has been raised in four places on a length of about 6 yards at each.

G.28.d.1.9, G.28.b.3.1, G.28.b.4.5 and G.28.b.4.6. appear to be particularly strong.

From G.28.b.4.6 to G.28.b.2.7 for 20 yards the parapet is low and wire in front is weak.

The isolated house at M.5.d.9.6 standing just behind the third line wire appears to have loopholed walls. A trench runs along the N.W. and S.W. sides with a communication trench leading Southwards to the embankment.

for Major General,

Commanding 47th (London) Division.

SECRET.   Copy No. 3
                          47th.(LONDON) DIVISION.

             BILLETS OCCUPIED BY UNITS ON EVENING OF MAY 25TH.1915.
                                                        June

Divisional Headquarters. (Less 3rd.Echelon). ..   ..   .. VERQUIN.
    3rd. Echelon.   ..   .. NOEUX-LES-MINES.
140th. Infantry Brigade.
    Headquarters.   ..   .. MAZINGARBE.
    6th. Bn. London Regt   ..   .. In trenches.
    7th.   "   "   (less 2 Companies)   ..   ..(MAZINGARBE.
    7th.   "   "   2 Companies.   ..   ..   ..(PHILOSOPHE.
    8th.   "   "   ..   .. PHILOSOPHE.
    15th. "   "   ..   .. In trenches.
    1st. Line Transport, 6th,7th,& 8th,Battalions. ..   .. NOEUX-LES-MINES.
    1st. Line Transport. 15th.Battalion..   ..   ..   .. HOUCHIN.
141st. Infantry Brigade.
    Headquarters.   ..   .. LES BREBIS.
    17th. Bn. London Regt.   ..   .. In trenches.
    18th. "   "   ..   .. LES BREBIS.
    19th. "   "   ..   .. In trenches.
    20th. "   "   ..   .. In trenches.
    1st. Line Transport of Brigade.   ..   .. HOUCHIN.
142nd. Infantry Brigade.
    Headquarters.   ..   .. NOEUX-LES-MINES.
    21st and 22nd. Bns. London Regt.   ..   .. MAZINGARBE.
    23rd and 24th.   "   "   ..   .. NOEUX-LES-MINES.
    1st. Line Transport of Brigade.   ..   .. HOUCHIN.
Divisional Mounted Troops.
    "C" Squadron, King Edward's Horse. ..   .. D.30.d.
    Cyclist Company.   ..   .. NOEUX-LES-MINES.
Divisional Artillery.
    Headquarters.   ..   .. MAZINGARBE.
    5th. London Bde.R.F.A.(less S.A.A.Section of B.A.C.) .. D.18.d.
    5th.   "   "   S.A.A.Section of B.A.C.   ..   .. DROUVIN WOOD.
    6th.   "   "   (Less 15th & 16th.Batteries   (South part of
                     and Brigade Ammunition Column) (LAPUGNOY.
    6th.   "   "   15th & 16th Batteries and
                     2/3rds.B.A.C.   ..   ..   .. Attached 2nd.Division.
    6th.   "   "   1 Gun Section & S.A.A.Section .. DROUVIN WOOD.
    7th.   "   "   (less 18th.Battery & S.A.A.   (South part of
                     Section of B.A.C).   ..   ..(LAPUGNOY.
    7th.   "   "   18th.Battery Wagon lines and
                     S.A.A.Section of B.A.C. ..   .. DROUVIN WOOD.
    8th. London (How) Brigade R.F.A.   ..   .. D.23.d.
    Divisional Ammunition Column.(Less 1 15pr Gun portion
                     and S.A.A.Portion).   ..   .. LAPUGNOY.
         "   "   1 15pr Gun portion & S.A.A.
                                portion   ..   ..   .. DROUVIN WOOD.
Divisional Engineers.
    Headquarters.   ..   .. MAZINGARBE.
    3rd. London Field Company R.E..   ..   .. LES BREBIS.
    4th. London Field Company R.E..   ..   .. MAZINGARBE.
    2/3rd. London Field Company R.E.   ..   .. NOEUX-LES-MINES.
Divisional Train.
    Headquarters & Hd.Qr.Company..   ..   .. D.30.c.
    Nos.2,3,and 4 Companies.   ..   .. Wood thro D.30.c.
Divisional Supply Column.   ..   .. E.3.b.

Divisional Medical Units.
    4th. London Field Ambulance. .. .. Chateau at DROUVIN.
    5th. " " " .. .. LE REVELLION.
    6th. " " " .. .. NOEUX-LES-MINES.
        with one Section. .. .. LES BREBIS.
        and Detachment. .. .. MAZINGARBE.
    Sanitary Section. .. .. NOEUX-LES-MINES.
    Motor Ambulance Workshop .. .. DROUVIN.

Mobile Veterinary Section.. .. .. HESDIGNEUL.E.26.d.
Convalescent Company. .. .. BETHUNE.

H.V. de la Fontaine

47 Div./S/25.
                            Major,
25th. June, 1915.
            D.A.A.& Q.M.G., 47th.(London) Division.

War Diary.

SECRET.　　　　47th (LONDON) DIVISION.　　　　Copy No. 2

OPERATION ORDER No. 10.

26th June, 1915.

1. The 142nd Inf.Bde. will relieve the 140th Inf.Bde. in Section "X" on the night of June 28th/29th, under arrangements to be made direct between G.O.C. 140th Inf. Bde. and O.C. 142nd Inf.Bde.

2. On relief, the 140th Inf.Bde. (less one battalion), will come into Divisional Reserve.

3. The G.O.C. 140th Inf.Bde. will place one Battalion at the disposal of O.C. 142nd Inf.Bde. for use as Brigade Reserve. This battalion, which will be billeted half at PHILOSOPHE and half at MAZINGARBE, will not be available for duty in the trenches.

4. Billets for 140th Inf.Bde., on relief, will be as follows :-

　　Hd.Qrs. and one battalion - NOEUX LES MINES.
　　Two battalions.　　　　　　- MAZINGARBE.

　　　　　　　　　　　　　　　　　　　Major,
　　　　　　　　　　　　　　　　　General Staff,
　　　　　　　　　　　　　　　　47th (Lon) Division.

Copies to - A.A.&.Q.M.G.,
　　　47th Divl.Mtd.Troops, 47th Div.Arty., 47th Div.Engrs.,
　　　47th Div.Sigs., 140th, 141st, 142nd Inf.Bdes.,
　　　47th Div.Train, 47th Div.Med., 1st Division and
　　　2nd Division, for information.

"C" Form (Duplicate).   **MESSAGES AND SIGNALS.**   Army Form C. 2123

No. DSH 25/26

Service Instructions: 2 addts Priority

TO: 47th Divn

Sender's Number	Day of Month	In reply to Number	AAA
19/N 56	26		

W3 Reports 4.40 pm Being shelled heavy shells in NORTH MAROC from direction of LENS

FROM: 141st Inf Bde
PLACE & TIME: 4.48 pm

War Diary.

47th Div.No.51/5.
26th June 1915.

47th (London) Division.

TACTICAL PROGRESS REPORT
up to noon 26th June 1915.

OPERATIONS. 1. Front line in W.3 shelled by heavy and light guns from 11 a.m. to 12.10 p.m. Five shells were blind.

WORK. 2. "W" Section. Wire improved. Work done on B Line. Trenches cleaned. Work continued on Keeps B, C & D.

"X" Section. Traversed fire trench from Sap 15 to 16 completed.
Fire trenches between Saps 13 and 14 and Saps 14 & 15 improved.
140 yards of wire single width erected between Saps 11 & 10. Wire is now continuous between these two points.
Sap 15 improved.
Chevaux de frise between Sap 14 and Trench 8 rewired.
Erection of overhead cover on Trench 12 continued.
Progress made on Keeps E, F, G and H.

INFORMATION. 3. A new loop is reported in communication trench at M.4.c.9.6.

From 20 yards South of M.4.c.1.8 to M.4.c.1.4 an overgrown ditch runs along the Western edge of road.

Six German Observation balloons up between LENS and LOOS at 6.15 p.m. (26th).

H R Hunt Capt
for Major General,
Commanding 47th (London) Division.

"C" Form (Duplicate).   Army Form C. 2123.
MESSAGES AND SIGNALS.   No. of Message

KA 70   Charges to Pay. £ s. d.   Office Stamp.

Service Instructions.

Handed in at **3LA** Office **10.22** m. Received **10.31** m.

TO **47 Div**

Sender's Number	Day of Month	In reply to Number	AAA
SC 146	27		

Following from OC XI begins
aaa Enemy are shelling centre
of our fire trench from
the direction of AUCHY - LEZ -
LA-BASSEE with high explosives aaa
The shells are falling about
fifty yards on the left
of the LENS Road and
are exploding on trench aaa
by are unable to see
the flash for hear the
report aaa ends aaa artillery
informed aaa

FROM PLACE & TIME   **140 Inf Bde**   **10-10 am**

W 9668/1672. 50,000 Pads. 12/14 A. W. & Co. Forms/C.2123.

"C" Form (Duplicate). Army Form C. 2123
MESSAGES AND SIGNALS. No. of Message...........

| | Charges to Pay. £ s. d. | Office Stamp. |

Service Instructions.
Handed in at... Priority 2LE ... Office 5.53 m. Received .... m.

TO 47th Lon Div

Sender's Number	Day of Month	In reply to Number	A A A
W1 falling from Div	report E. direction Arty	heavy end of informed	HE south LOOS	shells MAROC aaa

FROM PLACE & TIME 141st Inf Bde 5.50 PM

"C" Form (Duplicate).   Army Form C. 2193

MESSAGES AND SIGNALS.

From LPW 26   3LD Hill

| Service Instructions. | Charges to Pay. | Office Stamp. |

Handed in at ...FB... Office 11.13 a.m. Received 11.15 a.m.

TO 47 Div

Sender's Number	Day of Month	In reply to Number	AAA
M 9.50	28		

Heavy HE shells coming from
Direction of HAISNES bursting in
FOSSE no 7. aaa artillery
informed

700
11.15 a.m.

FROM 140 Inf Bde
PLACE & TIME 11.5 a.m.

"C" Form (Duplicate).   Army Form C. 2193.
MESSAGES AND SIGNALS. No. of Message...........

| | Charges to Pay. £ s. d. | Office Stamp. |

Service Instructions. *Priority*

Handed in at *ZLE*   Office *1.26* p.m. Received .... m.

TO *47th Div*

Sender's Number	Day of Month	In reply to Number	AAA
BM 96	28		

SOUTH MAROC being shelled 1.20 pm from direction of double CRASSIER

FROM *141st Inf Bde*
PLACE & TIME *1.25 pm*

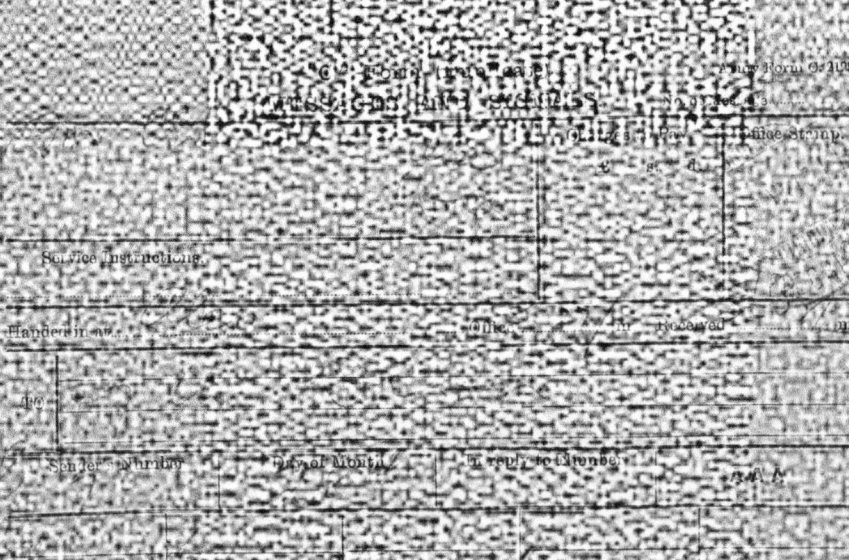

"C" Form (Duplicate). Army Form C. 2123
MESSAGES AND SIGNALS. No. of Message.

| | Charges to Pay. | Office-Stamp. |
| Priority at you | £ s. d. | [stamp: 28 VI 15] |

Service Instructions.

Handed in at 140 Office 4.0 p.m. Received 4.6 p.m.

TO 47 Div.

| Sender's Number | Day of Month | In reply to Number | AAA |
| S6.135 | 28 | | |

Enemy firing heavy shells into LE PHILOSOPHE appear trying to find 4.7 battery aaa

X

4.10 pm

FROM
PLACE & TIME 140 Inf Bde
4.0 pm

"C" Form (Duplicate). Army Form C. 2123
MESSAGES AND SIGNALS. No. of Message

	Charges to Pay.	Office Stamp.
3rd Copy for A/M/C aco Jn	£ s. d.	

Service Instructions.

Handed in at 1st Div. Office 4.30 p.m. Received 4.45 p.m.

TO 47 Divn.

Sender's Number	Day of Month	In reply to Number	AAA
G 512	28/6	1st Corps G7	

Shall be glad to retain for few days the two 15 pr. batteries at present attached to 2nd Divn aaa Joc. R.A. 1st Divn. will arrange details tomorrow with goc R.A. 47th. Divn addd 1st Corps repld 47th Divn 2nd Divn

FROM PLACE & TIME 1st Divn. 4.30 p.m.

"C" Form (Duplicate). Army Form C-2123.
MESSAGES AND SIGNALS.
No. of Message

	Charges to Pay.	Office Stamp.
Own LHrs 26 7hF Hills	£ s. d.	

Service Instructions.

Handed in at 7hF Office 11.55 p.m. Received 11.59 p.m.

TO 47th Div

Sender's Number	Day of Month	In reply to Number	AAA
Bm 106	28		
Distribution	tonight aaa		W1
17th Bn		W2	18th Bn
W3	19th Bn	Bde	Res
20th Bn			
		✗	
		72² 11·59 pm	

FROM 141st Inf Bde
PLACE & TIME 11·50 pm

Secret

War Diary

Copy No. 2

47th (LON) DIVISION OPERATION ORDER No. 11.

28th June, 1915.

1. The 1st Army will be re-organised as follows :-

   INDIAN Corps. . 51st, LAHORE, and MEERUT Divisions.

   First Corps. . 2nd, 7th, and 9th Divisions.

   Fourth Corps. . 1st, 47th, and 48th Divisions.

2. The 4th Corps is to take over the defensive front from the junction with the French up to and including "Z" Section.

3. The 1st Division relieves the 2nd Division in Sections "Y" and "Z"; the 3rd Brigade relieves the 5th Brigade in Section "Y" tonight.

4. The 47th (Lon) Division will continue to hold its present front and will come under the command of 4th Corps on the morning of June 30th.

5. The 15th and 16th (London) Field Batteries, with proportion of 8th (London) F.A.Brigade Ammunition Column, at present attached to 2nd Division, will remain in action and will be attached to the 1st Division; details of transfer being arranged between 1st and 2nd Divisions.

6. No. 5 Trench Mortar Battery (4"), at present with 7th Division, has been allotted to 47th (Lon) Division and is being transferred under arrangements made by 4th Corps.
   On arrival it will be allotted to "W" Section.

7. The 3rd Heavy Brigade R.G.A. will remain in its present position and be attached to 47th Division.

   The 15th R.M.A. Howitzer, and No. 17 Anti-aircraft Section, will remain attached to 47th (Lon) Division for administrative purposes.

   N.W.Webber.
   Major,
   General Staff,
   47th (London) Division.

Issued at 5-30 p.m. :-

   Copies to A.A.& Q.M.G., 47th Div.Mtd.Troops,
   47th Div.Arty., 47th Div.Engrs., 47th Div.Sigs,
   140th, 141st, and 142nd Inf.Bdes., 47th Div.
   Train, 47th Div.Med., and to 1st and 2nd
   Divisions for information.

Copy No.1 Op.Order File.
   2. War Diary.
   3 to 14 in order as given above.

War Diary

47th (London) Division.   47th Div. G/51/5
                                28th June 1915.

Tactical Progress Report
up to 12 Noon, June 28th 1915.

Operations. I. (a) Nil.

(b) Following points were shelled to-day :-

Fosse No. 7 at 11 a.m. with 5.9 c.m. shell from direction of CITE ST. ELIE.

Trenches in W.3 at 12, noon, from direction of M.5.d 85 and M.6.c 59; and again at 1 p.m. by battery believed to have been located in wood in S.E. corner of H.25.d.

Trenches on right of X.1 at 4.30 p.m.

Information. II. (i) Ground opposite M.9.d 57 is level, with grass 18" high. About 125 yards from our parapet are two rows of trip wire consisting of lines of semicircular loops about 12" diameter.
Sample of wire in front row herewith, second row ordinary barbed wire.
The main entanglement about this point consists of 3 rows, thickly interwoven.

(ii) Enemy working near Fosse No. 16.

(iii) Chevaux de frise put out at M.10.a 29.

(iv) Further observation of wire at M.4.a 64 shows that hostile patrols leave the German line at this point.

(v) German patrols were active opposite X.1 and enemy were working on a sap about G.28.c 61, with covering party in front.

(vi) Puits No. 14 Bis. (H.25.c 98) appears to be strongly fortified.

(vii) The parapet of the trench running North West through H.13.b 12 appears to be very high.

Work. III. Section W. Work continued on Keeps B and C. Also on new B Line behind MAISON DES MITRAILLEUSES.
Wiring completed between Saps 7 and 8.

Section X. Work continued on new fire trench joining Saps 14 and 15.
Work continued on Keeps E, F, G and H.
More wire put out round Sap 18.

N.W.Webber Major
for Major General,
Commanding 47th (London) Divn.

"A" Form. Army Form C. 2121.
MESSAGES AND SIGNALS.

TO: First Corps.
Advanced Second Div

Sender's Number: G.IN.113
Day of Month: 29th

AAA

Tactical Report AAA Situation normal AAA Relief of 140th Bde by 142nd Bde in Section X completed at 12-30 am AAA Addressed First Corps Repeated Advanced Second Div

From: 47th Div
Time: 5-5 am.

"C" Form (Duplicate). Army Form C. 2193.
MESSAGES AND SIGNALS.   No. of Message

For GK 22 aco
Howld

Service Instructions.

Handed in at "JDH" Office 7.50a.m. Received 8.15a.m.

TO 47th Divn

Sender's Number	Day of Month	In reply to Number	A A A
GB 57	29	—	

Headqtrs division closes BUSNES at 9 am and opens CHATEAU PHILOMEL u 22 a at same hour

728
8.18 am

FROM 48 Divn
PLACE & TIME

"C" Form (Duplicate).
MESSAGES AND SIGNALS.
Army Form C. 2123.

No. of Message.

Charges to Pay. £ s. d.

Office Stamp.

Service Instructions.

Handed in at .... Office .... m. Received .... m.

TO 47th Div

Sender's Number | Day of Month | In reply to Number
C47/8 | |

AAA

the Corps Commander will hold a conference at the old Chateau LA BUISSIERE at 2.30 pm tomorrow 30th June at which he wishes you to be present with your GSO 1st Grade and CRA aaa Acknowledge

FROM 4th Corps
PLACE & TIME 11.15 am

"C" Form (Duplicate).   Army Form C. 2123

MESSAGES AND SIGNALS.   No. of Message.

| DM hR 39 | aco Bray. | Charges to Pay. £ s. d. | Office Stamp. |

Service Instructions.

Handed in at **aco**   Office **11·50 a**m.   Received **1-8 p**m.

TO   4th Corps

Sender's Number	Day of Month	In reply to Number	AAA
G 4720	29th		

Reference 4th Corps operation order number 29 para 4 GOC 4th Corps will assume command of the new front at 12. NOON tomorrow aaa added First Army reptd all concerned

FROM / PLACE & TIME: 4th Corps 11-35 am

W.9668/1672. 50,000 Pads. 12/14 A. W. & Co. Forms/C.2123.

"C" Form (Duplicate).
MESSAGES AND SIGNALS.

Army Form C.2123
No. of Message ....

BMR 34 UCO
         Howe

Charges to Pay. £ s. d.   Office Stamp.

Service Instructions.

Handed in at UCO   Office 33 p.m.   Received 1.36 p.m.

TO 47th Div

Sender's Number	Day of Month	In reply to Number	AAA
G 25	29th		
1st Corps	report	Centre closes
at Chateau LA BUISSIERE at 3
pm and opens at Chateau
FILLETTE Choques same hour addressed
1st Army repeated all concerned
		✗	
(Copy handed A + Q)			
			73
			1.45 p.m

FROM 1st Corps
PLACE & TIME 1.30 pm

War Diary

47th Div No G/51/5.
29th June 1915.

47th (London) Division.

TACTICAL PROGRESS REPORT

up to noon 29th June 1915.

OPERATIONS. 1. (a) 142nd Bde relieved 140th Bde in Section "X": relief completed without incident.
  Hostile patrols opposite left of "W" 1 dispersed by trench mortars.

  (b) Nothing of interest to report.

INFORMATION. 2. A L.H.V. gun has been located behind a white tower N.E. of Puits No 15 (LOOS).

  Heliograph observed on bank S. of Puits No 15.

  Lamp signalling was observed between 10 p.m. & midnight last night on magnetic bearing 63° from S. point of Slag heap at Fosse No 6 (LES BREBIS).

  L.H.V. gun firing at 3.25 p.m. today from Red Roofed Building S. of Puits No 15. True bearing 77° from G.33.d.72

  Following gun targets were engaged by 3rd Heavy Bde R.G.A. yesterday:-
  A.30.b.63.
  H.14.a.32 - Flashes seen from Fosse No 9.
  H.26.c.99.
  A.30.b.10.0 - Battery seen from Fosse No 3. Observing Officer reports several shells appear effective.
  M.6.c.47.
  G.36.a.33.
  M.12.c.45.

WORK. 3. Section "W". Work continued on Keeps A & B.
  Wiring continued in front of "W" 3.

  Section "X". Improvement of new front trench between Saps 14 and 15 continued and trench wired.
  Keeps E, F and G will be permanently garrisoned tomorrow: wire, fire & communication trenches being completed.

            Major
        for Major General,
      Commanding 47th (London) Division.

"A" Form.
MESSAGES AND SIGNALS.

Army Form C. 2121.

TO: C.R.E. 4th Division

Sender's Number	Day of Month	In reply to Number	
W.R.132	30th		AAA

2/3 London Field Coy. R.E. less 1 Section will move to-morrow to Le Nushis to be employed under your orders on trench work. AAA The remaining section will continue work on well sinking AAA Please issue necessary orders & arrange billets at Le Nushis

From: 4th Division
Place:
Time: 10.50 pm

W Ruthven Lt Col

War Diary

47th Div. G/265/2
June 30th 1915

47th (London) Division.

INTELLIGENCE REPORT

for 24 Hours

Ending 12 Noon, Wednesday 30th June 1915.

(i) Men have been seen using Communication Trench M.4.d 14 - M.4.c 96.

(ii) Cyclists use road G.29.b 39 - G.29.d 44.

(iii) Several men seen to enter building at G.34.c 10.2.

(iv) Houses at Pit No. 16 are occupied.

(v) A trench exists running from M.6.c 2.7 through M.5.b 8.2 to G.35.c 7.5: it is wired on South West side: wire appears 4 feet high and 8 feet wide.

(vi) At 10.30 a.m. yesterday, the smoke of a train moving North was observed East of LOOS.

(vii) Smoke was seen rising from suspected Machine Gun Emplacement at G.28.b 4.5.

(viii) Front parapet G.22.d 5.0 - G.22.d 8.3 has been strengthened with sand bags and more loopholes made.

(ix) A line of strong high wire exists between fire and support trenches from G.22.d 7.1 to G.23.A 8.5. It probably extends further North but is not visible from our trenches.

(x) At G.23.a 4.2 the parapet is high and looks like a Machine Gun Emplacement.

(xi) From G.17.d 1.5 to G.17.b 5.1 front line wire is very strong and front and support line parapets high.

(xii) From head of Sap at G.17.a 9.4 trench runs North East and disappears behind thin fringe of trees at G.17.b 3.6. At this point wire can be seen behind front trench.

(xiii) Trench G.17.d 8.2 - G.17.d 9.9 has low parapet and looks disused.

(xiv) There are signs of wire entanglement at about G.18.b 82

(xv) There appears to be a strong post at G.11.b 3.4.

JWWebber Major
for Major General,
Commanding 47th (London) Division.

47th Div. G/265/3
30th June 1915.

47th (London) Division.

REPORT of work done and Summary of Operations during 24 hours ending Noon Wednesday 30th June, 1915.

OPERATIONS. I. (a) Following targets were engaged by 3rd Heavy Brigade, R. G. A. yesterday.

B.25.a 3.2.
A.30.b 8.2.

(b) Our Front Line and CRASSIER in W.2 were shelled intermittently during the morning by light and heavy guns.

WORK. II. Section W.

Work continued on Keep D.

Reconstruction of B Line on right of W.3 continued and 40 yards of wire entanglement put up on this line.

Work continued on shelters for Brigade Advanced Report Centre in CRASSIER.

Commenced new communication trench from railway cutting to ST. PANCRAS Road just West of Keep C.

Section X.

Work continued on Keeps E, F, G and H.

100 yards wire single width erected between Saps 15 and 16.

Work continued on communication trench between Saps 13 and 14 and on fire trench between Saps 14 and 15.

A.W.Webber Major

for

Major General,

Commanding 47th (London) Division

SECRET

Copy No. 4

OPERATION ORDER No. 29
BY
LIEUT.-GENERAL SIR H.S. RAWLINSON, Bt., K.C.B., C.V.O.,
COMMANDING IVth ARMY CORPS.

Head-quarters, IVth Army Corps.
26th June, 1915.

1. A further reconstitution of Corps has been decided upon and, on completion of the moves ordered below and on the march-table attached, the Corps of the 1st Army will consist of the following Divisions:-

<u>1st Corps</u> - 2nd, 7th, and 9th Divisions.
<u>IVth Corps</u> - 1st, 47th, and 48th Divisions.
<u>Indian Corps</u> - Meerut, Lahore, and 51st Divisions.

2. The IVth Corps will hold the line from the junction with the Xth French Army on the right to about CAMBRIN on the left, the 1st Corps continuing the line northwards as far as LA QUINQUE RUE with the Indian Corps on their left.

3. The IVth Corps line will be held by the 47th and 1st Divisions as follows:-

<u>47th Division</u>. Junction with Xth French Army to about LE RUTOIRE.
<u>1st Division</u>. About LE RUTOIRE to about CAMBRIN.
<u>48th Division</u>. In reserve.

Billeting areas as on map attached. *(Not attached) ksB*
Exact points of junction will be shown on a sketch map which will be forwarded later to Divisions concerned.
The 47th Division is already holding the above line.
The 1st Division will take over its section from the 2nd Division under orders issued by the 1st Corps.

4. The

4. The G.O.s C. 1st and IVth Corps will remain respons:ible for the present 1st and IVth Corps fronts until a time and date which will be communicated later.

5. The artillery of the 7th Division will remain res:ponsible for the defence of the new 1st Corps front from the Canal to LA QUINQUE RUE until other orders are issued by the 1st Corps.

6. The relief of the 153rd Infantry Brigade, now holding the line from about M.4 to LA QUINQUE RUE, will be carried out on the night of June 27th/28th by the 7th Division, instead of by the 49th Division as ordered in IVth Corps Operation Order No. 28 of the 23rd instant.

7. No. 2 Squadron, R.F.C., is moving, under arrange-ments made by the 1st Army, to near HESDIGNEUL for work with the IVth Corps.

8. No. 32 Anti-Aircraft Section will remain in its present area and will be attached to the 1st Corps (and not to the Indian Corps as previously ordered) from 6 a.m. on the 30th instant.

No. 17 Anti-Aircraft Section, now with the 1st Corps, will be transferred to the IVth Corps at the same time and date.

9. The 25th (Fortress) Co. R.E. will be attached temporarily to the 7th Division and will join the 47th Division on a date to be notified later.

10. The 176th Co. R.E. will remain attached to the 7th Division on transfer of that Division to the 1st Corps.

11. The/

11. The villages of OBLINGHEM and VENDIN LEZ BETHUNE are placed at the disposal of the 1st Corps from 6 p.m. on the 28th instant and will be clear of troops of the IVth Corps at that hour.

12. IVth Corps H.Q. will be established at LA BUISSIERE on the 30th instant.

13. Progress of moves and reliefs will be reported daily to 1st and IVth Corps Headquarters.

L. A. F. Bowly Capt.
for Brigadier General,
General Staff, IVth Corps.

Issued at _____

Copy No. 1 to 7th Division.
    "   2 to 51st Division.
    "   3 to 1st Division.
    "   4 to 47th Division.
    "   5 to 48th Division.
    "   6 to 146th Inf. Bde.
    "   7 to ~~Advanced~~ 1st Army.
    "   8 to Indian Corps.
    "   9 to 1st Corps.
    "   10 to IVth Corps and attached Artillery.
    "   11 to 1 Group H.A.R.
    "   12 to M.G. R.A. 1st Army.
    "   13 to D.A. & Q.M.G. IVth Corps.
    "   14 to No. 2 Sqdn. R.F.C.
    "   15 to IVth Corps File.
    "   16 to
    "   17 to
    "   18 to

Issued with 4thCorps O.O.29.

MARCH TABLE.

Formation.	Night of.	From.	Route.	To.	Remarks.
145th Infantry Bde.	27/28th	Area about GONNEHEM	LE REVEILLON - ALLOUAGNE	No.1 Billeting area.	To be South of the LILLERS - BETHUNE Railway by 8 p.m.
143rd Infantry Bde.	28/29th	Area about HAM-EN-ARTOIS	LILLERS.	No.2 Billeting area.	To be clear of LILLERS by 8 p.m.
144th Infantry Bde.	28/29th	VIEUX BERQUIN	MERVILLE - CALONNE - ROBECQ - LILLERS.	No.3 Billeting area.	

SECRET.   Copy No. 5

1st CORPS OPERATION ORDER No. 90.

                                        26th June, 1915.

1. The 1st Army will be re-organized as follows :-

      Indian Corps - 51st, Lahore, Meerut Divisions.
      1st Corps   - 2nd, 7th, 9th Divisions.
      4th Corps   - 1st, 47th, 48th Divisions.

2. 4th Corps will take over the defensive front from the junction with the French up to and including Section "Z".

3. 1st Corps will continue to hold the CUINCHY Section (A), and will take over the front from the 4th Corps north of the canal as far as LA QUINQUE RUE.

4. 1st and 4th Corps will retain command of their present fronts and areas, respectively, till morning of 30th June.

5. Preliminary moves will be carried out on 27th and 28th June as shewn in march table attached.
    All trench stores in Sections "Y" and "Z" will be handed over by 2nd Division to 1st Division.

6. (i) The relief of 2nd Divisional Artillery in Sections "Y" and "Z" by 1st Division will be carried out on nights of 29th and 30th June.
   (ii) The 3rd Heavy Brigade, R.G.A., and the 6th and 14th Siege Brigades, R.G.A., will remain in their present positions. The 3rd Heavy Brigade will be attached to 47th Division, and Headquarters and 2nd Battery of 6th Siege Brigade, R.G.A., will be attached to 1st Division from 29th June, inclusive.
        14th Siege Brigade and 5th Battery of 6th Siege Brigade will remain attached to 2nd Division.

7. The 9th Division will relieve the 7th Division (less artillery) in Section "C" (LE PLANTIN to LA QUINQUE RUE) on night 30th June-1st July, and 2nd Division will relieve remainder of 7th Division (less artillery) in Section "B" (GIVENCHY) on night 1st/2nd July.
    Further instructions will be issued regarding the artillery reliefs.

8. Secret Map "O" will be issued showing billeting areas of 1st Corps when the foregoing moves are completed.
    Daily progress of reliefs will be reported to 1st Corps.

                                    Rwlingham Brig. General.
                                        General Staff, 1st Corps.

Issued at 8:30 p.m. to :-
     1st Division.
     2nd Division.
     7th Division.
     9th Division.
    47th Division
     1st Group, H.A.R.
     Aeronautics 3.
     4th Corps.   For information.
     1st Army.   "   "

MARCH TABLE FOR MOVEMENTS - 27th and 28th JUNE 1915.

Formation.	Date.	Present area	Destination.	Route.	Remarks.
2nd Infantry Bde. 1st Division.	27/28th		Relieve 4th (Guards) Bde. in Section "Z".	GOSNAY—HESDIGNEUL— VAUDRICOURT—LABOURSE.	
4th (Guards) Bde. 2nd Division.	27/28th	Section "Z".	FOUQUIERES—FOUQUEREUIL and BETHUNE.	BEUVRY — BETHUNE.	To be clear of present area by 5 pm.27th.
25th Infantry Bde. 9th Division.	27/28th	FOUQUIERES—FOUQUEREUIL —ANNEZIN.	GONNEHEM—BUSNETTES— BAS RIEUX.	FOUQUEREUIL—CHOCQUES.	To be clear of FOUQUIERES - FOUQUEREUIL by 12 noon.
4th (Guards) Bde. 2nd Division.	28th.	FOUQUIERES—FOUQUEREUIL	OBLINGHEM - VENDIN and BETHUNE.	ANNEZIN.	
3rd Infantry Bde. 1st Division.	28/29th		Relieve 5th Inf.Bde. in Section "Y".	MARLES les MINES— LABUISSIERE—MOEUX les MINES.	
5th Infantry Bde. 2nd Division.	28/29th	Section "Y".	FOUQUIERES—FOUQUEREUIL ANNEZIN.	SAILLY LABOURSE— LABOURSE—VERQUIN and roads north thereof.	

1st Div
2nd Div
9th Div
47th Div

RW24   26th June

1. The 1st Army will be reorganized as follows:—

   Indian Corps = 51st, Lahore, Meerut Div
   1st Corps = 2nd 7th 9th Div.
   4th Corps = 1st 47th 48th Div.

2. 4th Corps will take over the defensive front from the junction with the Zouaves to left of 4th Guards Bde in Sections W X Y & Z.

3. 1st Corps will continue hold the CUINCHY Section (A) and will take over from the 4th Corps north of the Canal as far as LA QUINQUE RUE (the road and Mg incl).

   The following preliminary moves will take place on 27th & 28th

   (1) 1st Div will relieve 4th Guards Bde

in Section Z on Evening 27th.
(ii) 1st Div will relieve 5th Inf Bde in Section Y on Evening 28th.
(iii) 'A' Bde (with artillery bde attached) of 48th Div will move into ALLOUAGNE - LAPUGNOY - MARLES area as at present occupied by 1st Div at 6 pm 27th.
(iv) 'B' Bde (with attached troops) of 48th Div will move into AUCHEL area at 6 pm 28th.
(v) 'C' Bde (with attached troops) of 48th Div will move into ECQUEDECQUES - BURBURE area afternoon 28th.

4th Guards Bde on relief will move into Western & S.W. side of BETHUNE & ANNEZIN temporarily.
5th Inf Bde on relief will move into FOUQIERES - FOUQUEREN - ANNEZIN temporarily.
The areas of these brigades will be adjusted as billets North of CHOCQUES - BETHUNE road become available.
4th Bde will ~~probably~~ have to move out of ANNEZIN on

1. ~~Meaning~~ 28th to make way for 5th Bde.

6. Artillery relief between 1st & 2nd Divs will be carried out when infantry reliefs are complete

7. Eventually 2nd Div will relieve 7th Div in Givenchy Section as far N as K5 exclusive, and 9th Div will relieve 7th Div from K5 to La Quinque Rue. 7th Div will then be temporarily in reserve.

8. H.Q. 1st Corps will move to Chocques on Tuesday 29th and H.Q. 4th Corps will open at La Buissière on Wed'y 30th.

9. Hesdigneul & Gosnay are reserved by 4th Corps orders

"A" Form.   Army Form C. 2121.

MESSAGES AND SIGNALS.

Prefix	Code	m.	Words	Charge	This message is on a/c of:	Recd. at _____ m.
Office of Origin and Service Instructions.			Sent			Date _____
Secret S.D.R.			At _____ m.		_____ Service.	From _____
			To _____			By _____
			By _____		(Signature of "Franking Officer.")	

TO Adm 1st Div / 2nd Div / 47th Div

Sender's Number: G.987   Day of Month: 27   In reply to Number: AAA

In continuation of 1st Corps operation Order No 90 of June 28th the 1st Guards Brigade will move tomorrow from BURBURE and HURIONVILLE to YERQUIN - VAUDRICOURT - LABEUVRIERE - GOSNAY and HESDIGNEUL aaa Route ALLOUAGNE - LAPUGNOY - GOSNAY - HESDIGNEUL aaa Troops remaining in GOSNAY and HESDIGNEUL are not to be dispossessed aaa addressed 1st Div repeated Advanced 2nd Div & 47th Div.

From: 1st Corps
Place:
Time: 7.40 p.m.

SEA Bond
Major for
BGGS 1st Corps

S E C R E T.   Copy No. 5

1st CORPS OPERATION ORDER No. 91.

27th June, 1915.

1. In continuation of 1st Corps Operation Order No. 90, dated 26th June, 1915, the following units will form part of the 1st Corps :-

Unit.	Attached to.
3rd Squadron, R.F.C.	Corps Troops.
No. 7 Mountain Battery, R.G.A.	2nd Division.
Motor Machine Gun Battery	2nd Division.
No. 11 Anti-Aircraft Section	Corps Troops.
No. 22 Anti-Aircraft Section	Corps Troops.
No. 6 Trench Mortar Battery, 1½"	2nd Division.
No. 1 Trench Mortar Battery, 1½"	7th Division.
No.10 Trench Mortar Battery, 2"	7th Division.
No. 9 Trench Mortar Battery, 1½"	9th Division.
170th Co.R.E.(for work in CUINCHY Section)	2nd Division.
176th Co.R.E.(for work in GIVENCHY Section)	7th Division.
Hants Fortress Company, R.E.	Corps Troops.
31st Fortress Company, R.E.	Corps Troops.

2. The following units will be attached to 1st Corps :-

14th Siege Brigade, R.G.A. (9th & 11th Batteries)	2nd Division.
5th Siege Battery, R.G.A.	2nd Division.
2nd Brigade, R.G.A. (26th & 35th Heavy Batteries, 2nd London Heavy Battery)	2nd Division.) For
40th Balloon Company (French)	2nd Division.)adm'n.
R.N.V.R. 3-pr Armoured Cars	Corps Troops.
Graves Commission	2nd Division.) For
Hospital Barges	2nd Division.)adm'n.
Siege Ammunition Parks	Corps Troops.
No. 9 Ammunition Park	Corps Troops.

3. The following units will be transferred for administrative purposes as follows :-

Left Section of 15th Battery 9.2"	to 1st Division from 30th incl.
15" R.M.A. Howitzer	to 47th Division from 30th incl.
No. 17 Anti-Aircraft Section	to 47th Division from 30th incl.
47th Ammunition Park	to Corps Troops 4th Corps from 30th inclusive.

R W Ingham Brig. General.
General Staff, 1st Corps.

Issued at 10 a.m. to :-

    1st Division.
    2nd Division.
    7th Division.
    9th Division.
    47th Division.
    1st Group, H.A.R.
    No. 3 Squadron, R.F.C.
    4th Corps.   For information.
    1st Army   For information.
    Indian Corps. For information.

SECRET Copy No. 5

OPERATION ORDER No: 30
BY
LIEUT: GENERAL SIR H.S.RAWLINSON, Bt., K.C.B. C.V.O.,
COMMANDING 4th ARMY CORPS.

Headquarters, IVth Corps,
27th June, 1915.

1. With reference to Operation Order No. 29 of 26th instant, the following reallotment and transfer of trench mortar batteries will take place on the reconstitution of the 4th Corps :-

(a) <u>Transfer - 4th Corps to 1st Corps.</u>

No. 1 Battery (1½")) With 7th Division.
No.10 ,, (2"))
No. 9 ,, (1½") - With 9th Division.

(b) <u>Transfer - 1st Corps to 4th Corps.</u>

No.12 Battery (1½") - With 47th Division.
No. 7 ,, (2") - With 1st Division.

(c) <u>Future allotment of 4th Corps Batteries.</u>

No. 2 Battery (1½")) 1st Division.
No. 7 ,, (2"))
No. 3 ,, (4")) 47th Division.
No.12 ,, (1½"))
No. 8 ,, (1½") - 46th Division.

2. The 7th Division will arrange to send Nos. 2, 3 and 8 Batteries to the Divisional Ammunition Column, LES CHOCQUAUX on the 28th instant where they will be taken over under arrangements by the A.Q.M.G., 4th Corps for distribution as in paragraph (c) above.

A.G.Dallas
Brigadier General.
General Staff, IVth Corps.

Issued at 12 hours

Copies to /

Copy No. 1 to 1st Army.
" 2 to 1st Corps.
" 3 to 7th Division.
" 4 to 9th Division.
" 5 to 47th Division.
" 6 to 1st Division.
" 7 to 48th Division.
" 8 to D.A. & Q.M.G., 4th Corps.
" 9 to 4th Corps file.
" 10 to Indian Corps.
" 11 to
" 12 to

SECRET.   Copy No. 5

1st CORPS OPERATION ORDER No. 92.

Reference map 1/10,000.   29th June, 1915.

1. In continuation of para. 7 of 1st Corps Operation Order No. 90 the relief of infantry of 7th Division by infantry of 2nd and 9th Divisions will be carried out as follows :-

   (i) 5th Infantry Brigade, 2nd Division, will relieve 20th (Guards) Brigade in GIVENCHY Section night 30th June - 1st July.
   (ii) 26th Infantry Brigade, 9th Division, will relieve 21st Infantry Brigade from M.4. inclusive to junction with Indian Corps at LA QUINQUE RUE on night 30th June-1st July.
   (iii) 27th Infantry Brigade, 9th Division, will relieve 22nd Infantry Brigade from J.7. inclusive to M.4. exclusive on night 1st/2nd July.

2. (i) The relief of 7th Divisional Artillery covering GIVENCHY Section by 2nd Divisional Artillery will be carried out on nights 1st/2nd and 2nd/3rd July, so as to be completed by 6 a.m. 3rd July.
   (ii) The relief of the remainder of 7th Divisional Artillery by artillery of 9th Division will proceed as previously arranged, so as to be completed by 6 a.m. 2nd July.

3. (i) G.O.C. 2nd Division, Headquarters BETHUNE, will assume command of GIVENCHY Section, including artillery, at 6 a.m. 1st July.
   (ii) G.O.C. 9th Division, Headquarters LOCON, will assume command of the defensive front J.7 (inclusive) to junction with Indian Corps at 6 a.m. 2nd July.

4. Sections of defence north of the canal will be designated as follows :-
   GIVENCHY................... Section "B".
   J.7. to M.4................ Section "C".
   M.4. to LA QUINQUE RUE..... Section "D".

5. (i) No. 3 Trench Mortar Battery at present in action at "THE ORCHARD" (M.9.) will remain at disposal of 9th Division till Saturday, 3rd July, when it is to be handed over to 47th Division under arrangements to be made direct with that division.
   (ii) 7th Division will leave the mortars of its two trench mortar batteries at disposal of 2nd Division in Section "B", and 9th Division in Section "C" respectively.

                                              R.Whigham Brig. General.
                                              General Staff, 1st Corps.

Issued at 1:30 p.m. to :-
    1st Division.
    2nd Division.
    7th Division.
    9th Division.
    47th Division.
    Aeronautics 3.
    1st Group, H.A.R.)
    4th Corps.   )
    Indian Corps.   ) For information.
    1st Army.   )

Reconnaissance Work

47th Division.

No. Misc. 8.   29th June, 1915.

" The Lieut. General Commanding 1st Corps desires to place on record his appreciation of the excellent reconnaissance work done by Lieut. H.T. Lewis, 15th Battn. London Regiment (Civil Service Rifles).

The clear and concise reports on the enemy's positions sent in by this officer are most useful. "

R. Whigham Brig. General.
General Staff, 1st Corps.

Routine Orders 1/7/15